MONITORING THE OUTCOMES OF SOCIAL SERVICES VOLUME I:
Preliminary Suggestions

ANNIE MILLAR
HARRY HATRY
MARGO KOSS

5039-2
MAY 1977

THE URBAN INSTITUTE
WASHINGTON, D.C.

This work has been supported by the U.S. Department of Health, Education and Welfare, and the National Center for Productivity and Quality of Working Life. In addition, the states of North Carolina and Wisconsin have been active participants in various portions of this work. The views expressed herein are those of the authors and do not necessarily reflect those of these other agencies.

ISBN 87766-194-4

UI 5039-1

PLEASE REFER TO URI 19100 WHEN ORDERING

Available from:

Publications Office
The Urban Institute
2100 M Street, N. W.
Washington, D. C. 20037

List price: $4.00

A/77/3M

PREFACE

This two-volume report on procedures for monitoring social services outcomes is one of a series of reports about ways to measure the outcomes of basic state government services. The other reports deal with mental health services, chronic disease control programs, corrections, economic development, and transportation.

Concerned citizens and government officials--in particular, service agency personnel, budget and planning staffs, legislators, and gubernatorial staff--have become increasingly concerned about the effectiveness of government services. Little useful information is currently available on the effectiveness of such services in meeting the needs of their clientele. The research leading to this series of reports was, therefore, undertaken as an initial step toward developing procedures that would enable jurisdictions to obtain such information. Though the work was initially directed at helping state governments, the material also appears to be quite appropriate for utilization by local agencies.

This series of reports is an initial effort in what is a very large task. Several of the procedures outlined in the reports need considerable development--steps that may require the investment of significant financial and staff resources. Despite its exploratory character, the work completed thus far indicates that considerably improved effectiveness information can be made available.

This work focuses on the outcomes (or end results) of services to be monitored by a state or local agency on a regular basis and on the procedures for collecting data on these outcomes. Such data, collected over a period of time, can indicate trends, progress and problems. Consequently, outcome information is an important aid to public officials and concerned citizens for finding out just what is being accomplished and for identifying areas that need extensive examination.

These procedures are, however, no substitute for program evaluation methods (such as "controlled" experiments and sophisticated techniques of statistical analysis) that attempt to identify specific effects of specific programs.

The research that led to these reports was carried out by The Urban Institute and the states of North Carolina and Wisconsin, with the cooperation of the National Association of State Budget Officers. The National Center for Productivity and Quality of Working Life, the U.S. Department of Health, Education, and Welfare, the U.S. Department of Transportation, and the Ford Foundation have provided financial support for these efforts. The primary support for this volume was the U.S. Department of Health, Education, and Welfare.

We hope that these reports will increase awareness of the information needed to reflect citizen and client concerns regarding public services, encourage state and local governments to consider, develop, and use these or similar measurement procedures, and stimulate further research and developmental efforts to produce reliable outcome measurement techniques.

CONTENTS

CONTENTS

ACKNOWLEDGMENTS

The North Carolina Department of Human Resources-Division of Social Services Program Evaluation Task Force played a major role in the development of the ideas discussed in this report. In particular, Sandy Brenneman and Len Farrar of the Management Assistance Section, Division of Plans and Programs, and Ronald Penney of the Division of Social Services were major participants. In addition, Gloria Grizzle, Barbara Matula, and Richard Rideout from the Department of Administration of the state of North Carolina also participated in the planning and review of the project efforts. William Benton and Jerry Turem of The Urban Institute provided invaluable advice throughout the project.

From the state of Wisconsin, Bernie Mrazik of the Department of Administration, and Jack Christian, Sam Moore, and Stuart Morse of the Department of Health and Social Services, provided suggestions at various stages of the work and were major participants in the Wisconsin test of the use of citizen surveys for assessing unmet needs.

In addition, Patricia Vucich, an intern from Michigan State University, provided helpful input, as did Michael Lugar of the University of California at Berkeley.

We are also grateful for the suggestions and reviews of draft reports of a number of advisors to the project. These include:

Norman G. Angus
Department of Social Services
State of Utah

Walter Balk
State University of New York
   at Albany

Pat Barrett
United Way of America

George A. Bell
National Association of State
   Budget Officers

Charles F. Cain
U.S. Department of Health, Education
   and Welfare, Region IV

Vee Carnall
U.S. Department of Health, Education
   and Welfare, Region V

Reginald Carter
Department of Social Services
State of Michigan

Thomas Coyle
U.S. Department of Health, Education
   and Welfare

Libby Halperin
U.S. Department of Health, Education
and Welfare, Region V

Nancy Hayward
National Center for Productivity
and Quality of Working Life

Jerry Hercenberg
United Way of America

Allen Holmes
Department of Budget and Fiscal
Planning
State of Maryland

J. Donald Judy
National Association of State
Budget Officers

Dr. Sidney Katz
Michigan State University College
of Human Medicine

Laura Kemp
Department of Social and Health
Services
State of Washington

Kynoch Kendall
Social and Rehabilitation Service
U.S. Department of Health, Education
and Welfare

Thomas E. Lavelle
Department of Administration
State of Minnesota

Don Murray
National Association of Counties

Ray Pethtel
Joint Legislative Audit and Review
Commission
State of Virginia

Patrick V. Riley
Family Services Association of
Greater Boston

Alfred Schainblatt
The Urban Institute

Jerry Silverman
U.S. Department of Health, Education
and Welfare

Iris Slack
American Public Welfare Association

Michael Springer
The Urban Institute

Sylvia Vela
Social and Rehabilitation Service
U.S. Department of Health, Education
and Welfare

Catherine G. Williams
Department of Social Services
State of Iowa

David Wilson
U.S. Department of Health, Education
and Welfare

Suzanne Woolsey
The Urban Institute

SUMMARY

Administrators and program planners at the state and local level have
become increasingly concerned about the dearth of comprehensive information
on the effects of social service programs. Such information seems vital for
informed program and policy formulation.

Current evaluation work tends to concentrate on one-time studies, usually of specific programs or specific services. Regular performance assessment
efforts tend to focus on such measures of administrative activity as "number
of persons served" or "number of interviews conducted." There is little
evidence of regular follow-up studies to assess the impact of programs on
clients at some interval after clients receive social services.

It is our belief, however, that state and local governments can make
some meaningful beginning efforts to collect comprehensive data on the effects of social services on clients. Hence, this report discusses a preliminary set of data collection procedures for monitoring the outcomes of social
service programs.

These procedures are intended to provide annual measurements of outcomes
for use by state officials in governors' offices, in state budget and planning
offices, and in state legislatures, as well as in state social service agencies. Much of the discussion in this report and the procedures described
also appear to be applicable for local agency use. The client sample sizes
suggested in this report as minimum samples for state governments are not
large enough to yield sufficiently precise information to administrators at
the county level on the effectiveness of county-level social services, except
perhaps in a few of the largest counties. Thus, most county officials seeking
to adapt these procedures for their own purposes will find it necessary to
collect additional samples. At the local community level, caseworkers may
find parts of the procedures adaptable for their own individual assessments,
but such adaptation is not discussed in this report.

The Scope of This Study

This study focuses on social services, such as those funded under Title
XX of the Social Security Act. Income maintenance programs are not included.
The suggested outcome monitoring procedures aim at assessing:

1. The functioning level of clients after receipt of social services,
   preferably as related to their status at the time they began to

receive services (referred to subsequently as "entry" or "intake"). If assessments are made for each client at two different times, the amount of change in each client's condition can be identified.

2. The degree of client satisfaction with the services received.

3. The amount of unmet need in the state (or county), that is, the extent to which there are citizens who need social services who are not currently receiving them.

The procedures discussed here are not intended to replace in-depth program evaluation efforts designed to determine the amount of client change that can be attributed to specific programs. Unlike efforts of that type, outcome monitoring will not, by itself, permit definitive statements to the effect that changes in clients' conditions are the direct result of specific services. But the three kinds of assessments listed above can provide at least a gross indication of the results following major changes in the provision of social services. In addition, such monitoring, conducted regularly, can help:

-Indicate trends in outcomes over a period of time.

-Identify problem areas that need management attention.

-Assist in resource allocation by identifying budget needs and justifying budget requests.

-Indicate areas where in-depth program evaluation would be desirable.

-Provide representative client and citizen feedback to government officials on a periodic basis.

-Increase the accountability of social service agencies to governors, legislators, and the general public.[1]

This study is not intended to be a definitive work on monitoring the outcome of social services. Since the procedures discussed have not been adequately tested, it should be considered an exploratory effort. A state (or local) agency that intends to use these procedures will have to conduct testing prior to full-scale implementation.

Since the recipients of social services often have multiple problems, the focus here is on the individual client "as a whole" and on the range of the client's needs, as distinguished from emphasizing a "primary" goal or a particular service that was provided. The procedures are therefore not service-specific; they do not aim at providing measurements of outcome for each of the many individual social service programs. If information on the type and amount of service is obtained for each client in a sample, however, the outcomes can be analyzed in relation to specific services or combinations of services. And if major service changes are made, subsequent monitoring of outcomes will provide at least a crude indication of the results of those changes.

_____

1. See Chapter 6 for more discussion of the uses of information on outcomes.

Research Undertaken for This Study

This report is based on several research steps:

1. An intensive search for studies, evaluations, and needs assessments conducted by state and county social service departments, by public and private agencies, and by professional organizations. This involved the examination of literature and procedures that have been used (generally in ad hoc studies) as well as telephone and personal conversations with practitioners and researchers in the field.[1]

2. Identification of various "indicators" of client status at any given time based on the information obtained in step 1 and discussions with state social service personnel.[2]

3. The development and, where possible, adaptation from instruments developed by others of questions that elicit information on client status.

4. Participation in the development and pretesting of a state's client outcome evaluation questionnaire.

5. Participation in the development of a set of questions to assess the unmet need for social services within a state.[3]

A considerable portion of this effort was a cooperative venture between The Urban Institute and the states of North Carolina and Wisconsin to develop procedures and, where possible, to test them. In North Carolina, a questionnaire for assessing client change and client satisfaction (similar to the one provided in Appendix A) was pre-tested. In Wisconsin, an initial effort was undertaken to survey a sample of state citizens to provide rough estimates of unmet need for social services, as part of a multi-service survey effort.

Principal Procedures Recommended

Two principal procedures are recommended as a regular--preferably annual--undertaking:

----

1. The second volume of this report, Monitoring the Outcomes of Social Services, Volume II: A Review of Past Research and Test Activities, describes our findings.

2. This step and steps 3 and 4 were carried out in cooperation with the Program Evaluation Task Force, Division of Social Services, of the state of North Carolina. The task force consisted of members of the evaluation unit of the Department of Human Resources, personnel from the Division of Social Services, and members of the budget and planning offices of the Department of Administration.

3. This step was carried out in cooperation with the Wisconsin state government for inclusion in that state's 1976 multi-service statewide citizen survey.

1. A survey of a random sample of clients, perhaps 2,000 to 3,000. These clients would be surveyed both at (or near) entry, and at some fixed interval (such as twelve months) thereafter. For each sampled client, information would be sought on a number of indicators of (a) the client's ability to function, so that degree of improvement (or maintenance of functioning where major chronic problems existed) could be estimated; (b) the client's own perception of the amount of change effected; and (c) the client's satisfaction with the services received.

This information would be obtained chiefly from clients themselves, but in some instances (such as for the very young or those unable to respond for themselves) from others closely acquainted with the clients. Selected items, such as child placement data, would be obtained from government records.

2. A survey of a cross section of households in the state (or, if undertaken by a county agency, in the county) to estimate the extent to which there are citizens who need social services who are not being served. This measurement of the magnitude of "unmet need" would involve from 1,500 to 2,000 households.

Specific Information To Be Obtained (Chapters 1, 2, and 5)

Exhibit 1 lists thirty indicators of client outcomes and unmet citizen need identified for regular monitoring. These indicators can be grouped into twelve categories, hereafter referred to as "dimensions." These dimensions are:

(1) Economic self-support
(2) Ability to undertake the activities of daily living
(3) Physical health
(4) Mental distress
(5) Alcohol and drug abuse
(6) Family strength
(7) Child problem behavior
(8) Child welfare
(9) Client satisfaction
(10) Amenities of care in institutions
(11) Appropriateness of care
(12) Unmet need of citizens for social services.

Information on each of the first eleven dimensions would come in whole or in part from the annual survey of a sample of clients. Information on the last dimension, unmet need, would be obtained from the survey of a sample of households within a government's jurisdiction.

Appendix A presents a preliminary data collection instrument for the client outcome indicators, and Appendix B presents a preliminary data collection instrument for unmet need indicators.

Exhibit 1 also indicates which questions on the instruments are suggested to obtain the information for each indicator. As the exhibit shows, most of the indicators are based on information obtained from more than one question.

EXHIBIT 1

A LIST OF INDICATORS OF THE OUTCOMES OF SOCIAL SERVICES
(INCLUDING CLIENT OUTCOMES AND THE UNMET NEED OF CITIZENS)

CLIENT OUTCOMES

	Questions in Appendix A*
Economic Self-Support	
1. Current employment status	1
2. Length of time employed in three-month period prior to interview	2
3. Quality of jobs held	3
4. Amount earned in three-month period	4
5. Extent of dependence on public assistance	5
Ability to Undertake the Activities of Daily Living	
6. Level of functioning on activities of daily living	6-18
Physical Health	
7. Number of days restricted activity during the past three months	19-20 & R-1
8. Overall health as perceived by the client	21-22
9. Client's perception of degree of improvement since receiving services	23
Mental Distress	
10. Index of mental distress	24-33
11. Indication of major mental depression	34-36 & R-2,3
12. Degree of loneliness/isolation	37-39
13. Overall attitude toward life in general	40
14. Client's perception of degree of improvement since receiving services	41
Alcohol and Drug Abuse	
15. Extent of alcohol abuse	42-47 & R-4
16. Extent of drug abuse	48-53 & R-5
Family Strength	
17. Extent of family problems	54-63
18. Client's perception of degree of improvement since receiving services	64-74
Child Problem Behavior	
19. Extent of child behavior problems	75-85
20. Respondent's perception of degree of improvement since receiving services	86-92
Child Welfare	
21. Child abuse recidivism	R-6
22. Timeliness of placement	R-7
23. Improvement in child's living situation	R-8
Client Satisfaction	
24. Client's perception of degree of overall improvement since receiving services	94
25. Client's perception of the degree to which services have helped	95
26. Client's satisfaction with various aspects of services provided (for example, fees, location of agency, waiting time, etc.)	96-104
Amenities of Care in Institutions	
27. Client's satisfaction with services provided in the institution	105-122
Appropriateness of Care	
28. Percentage of clients currently in institutions who appear to be inappropriately placed	See Chapter 2
29. Percentage of clients not in institutions who appear to need institutional care	See Chapter 2

UNMET NEED OF CITIZENS FOR SOCIAL SERVICES	Questions in Appendix B
30. Percentage of respondents indicating that someone in their household had unmet need for help with at least one social-service-related problem**	1-17

---

*Numbers prefaced by an "R" are items to be obtained from case records (see Appendix A).
**This is an aggregate indicator; for each individual problem there is an indicator, stated as follows: percentage of respondents who felt that someone in their household had the problem, but either did not seek help, for reasons that the government could have influenced, or sought help and did not receive it, for reasons that the government could have influenced.

In effect, a number of perspectives are obtained for each. The specific questions and their rationale are discussed in Chapters 1 and 5. It is likely that each state (or local government) will want to modify the outcome information to be obtained. Dimensions, indicators, and questions can be added, deleted, or altered when this appears desirable.

The "appropriateness of care" dimension presents special complexities that are discussed in greater detail in Chapter 2. This dimension can in part be assessed by using information from a number of the other dimensions, as well as supplementary information such as on the availability of services.

To assess outcomes on the five individual goals for social services listed under Title XX the various dimensions listed above would be used. Dimension 1 would provide information needed to assess Goal 1 (economic self-support); Dimensions 2 through 5 would provide information needed to assess Goal 2 (self-sufficiency); Dimensions 6 through 8 would provide information needed to assess Goal 3 (preventing abuse and strengthening families); a number of dimensions, along with supplementary information, would provide the information needed to assess Goal 4 (avoiding inappropriate institutional care); and a number of dimensions, along with unmet need data, would provide the information needed to assess Goal 5 (providing institutional care for those in need).

Client satisfaction seems implicitly relevant to all five goals. Client satisfaction is defined here to include both clients' perceptions of their overall improvement and their satisfaction with such specific matters as accessibility of the services and the courtesy with which services were rendered.

Clients' perceptions of whether the services they received were satisfactory are increasingly recognized as important, even when these perceptions appear to conflict with "objective" indicators of change. Explicit indications of client satisfaction therefore appear desirable. Such information can be readily obtained during follow-up interviews.

How Is Client Outcome Information To Be Obtained?   (Chapters 2, 3 and 4)

The principal procedure suggested for the collection of data is a structured interview with a representative sample of clients drawn each year. The client questionnaire would be administered at, or near, the time at which clients begin to receive services and again at some period after they have received social services. (Information on client satisfaction, of course, would be sought only after the receipt of services.)

Not all the information indicated in Exhibit 1 needs to be obtained for all types of clients. Only the information that appears appropriate for each type of client would be obtained. For example, adult clients without children would not be queried on child behavior problems. (Preliminary suggestions as to which sections of the questionnaire would be applicable to various types of clients are presented in Chapter 2.)

There are several issues related to sampling clients that each state will have to resolve for itself. Since funds for these assessments are likely to be limited, states will be able to sample no more than perhaps 2,000 to 3,000 clients each year. Thus, an important task will be to determine the major categories of clients for which statistically representative information is most needed. Some of the more obvious categories are clients residing in various geographical areas, clients with different primary goals, and clients with different types of problems. To achieve at least minimum precision, samples of at least 100 clients are recommended for each category. Obtaining an up-to-date list of clients from which to draw the sample is likely to be a problem in many states. However, a "perfect" list is not essential; one that provides rough coverage of all categories of clients of interest should be sufficient. These and other sampling questions should be resolved in pilot tests of the procedures. These tests should be conducted before full-scale implementation is undertaken.

Another major question is the mode of interviewing (mail, telephone, in-person, or some combination) to be adopted. In-person interviewing probably would permit the greatest accuracy, but it is by far the most costly approach. Tests of mail/telephone/in-person combinations are desirable in order to determine if the number and quality of responses are satisfactory enough to obviate the need for all interviews to be in-person. Even when in-person interviews are necessary, mail and telephone can be used to locate clients or ex-clients, thereby reducing costs.

Another important question is the selection of interviewers. In order to avoid bias or lack of credibility, the client's own caseworker probably should not be used. Moreover, the added burden on caseworkers (especially for those follow-up interviews for clients that had terminated services) would be substantial. Another major problem would be assuring the quality of the assessments if large numbers (perhaps hundreds) of caseworkers were involved. For these reasons, it is recommended that a small group of trained interviewers be used.

At What Interval Should Client Outcome Information Be Obtained? (Chapter 3)

As already mentioned, assessments of change in the condition of clients can be made if the state obtains information on clients both at intake and at some interval after receiving services. The point at which the follow-up should be undertaken thus becomes a critical matter. If the follow-ups are done at the time cases are closed, little information will be provided as to the lasting effects of social services because the ability of clients to be truly self-supporting or self-sufficient will probably not be observable so early.

Ideally, follow-up should be undertaken at some point after case closure, such as nine or twelve months. The longer a client's case has been closed, however, the harder and more expensive it becomes to locate the client for the follow-up interview. Another problem is that some clients are in the social service system for many years; hence, waiting until case closure excludes these clients from the sample indefinitely.

It is suggested here that the follow-up assessment be conducted at some fixed interval after intake, such as twelve months. This permits assessment of the "percentage of clients showing various degrees of improvement twelve months after intake into the social service system." Referencing the follow-up to the time of intake is procedurally convenient and will likely provide adequate post-service information. Some clients will still be receiving services at the time of follow-up; some will not. Each year a new sample of clients would be selected for monitoring from the total number of incoming clients. It may also be appropriate to sample each year those clients who have been receiving social services for extended periods of time.

Information obtained at intake also provides a way to classify clients according to "difficulty." Such categorization can make interpretation of client-change data considerably more meaningful. For example, it allows public officials to estimate the extent to which success, or lack of it, is due to a change in the clientele (for example, a significantly higher percentage of clients with more severe conditions) rather than to the services provided.

Estimating the Extent of Unmet Need for Social Services (Chapter 5)

In addition to the client outcome-monitoring procedure, an annual survey of a representative sample of a state's (or county's) citizens is needed to provide estimates on the number of citizens who perceive themselves as having a social-service-related problem but who have either not sought help or have sought help and not received it, especially for reasons that the state has at least partial responsibility to try to alleviate. Some examples of such reasons for not obtaining help are: lack of information on available help, inaccessibility, and lack of temporary child care. The survey should attempt to identify which reasons apply.

Surveys to obtain information on needs have been undertaken on an ad hoc basis by a number of states. It is suggested here that a set of questions (such as those shown in Appendix B) be included in a state multi-service citizen survey, such as those recently tested by the states of Wisconsin and North Carolina. This type of survey would obtain information on a number of other services (such as health, transportation, employment, and recreation) in addition to social services.

Some Implementation Issues (Chapter 7)

Activities such as the following should be undertaken to help achieve a relatively smooth implementation of state outcome-monitoring procedures.

1. Substantial participation by representatives of state program offices, personnel from county and regional agencies, and representatives of interested private agencies, all of whom will act both as data sources and as users of information.

2. Careful planning and gradual phasing-in of procedures, in order to reduce anxiety and disruptions and ensure cooperation.

3. Careful delineation of how outcome monitoring information will be used. This should include assurances that the procedures will not be used to evaluate the performance of individual caseworkers, that the privacy and confidentiality of data about individual clients will be observed (data should be provided to users only in aggregate form), and, if undertaken by a state government, that the information obtained will not be used to tell local social service agencies, public or private, how to run their operations or what they have to do.

4. Establishing some degree of flexibility in procedures in order to permit change.

5. Coordination with those responsible for the formal (often computerized) social service reporting systems (such as those for the federal government's social service reporting requirements). Such coordination will help avoid misunderstandings as to the impact of the procedures on such reporting systems. The proposed procedures should not require any revamping of reporting systems. The client outcome monitoring procedures are likely to be users of existing computer information for various purposes, such as drawing the sample of clients.

6. Provision of substantial analytical resources, initially to help develop the data collection procedures and the formats for presenting the data to users, and subsequently (on an annual basis) to analyze the data so that the information will be as meaningful and useful as possible. Exhibit 2 provides an illustration of the way outcome information might be summarized for public officials.

Summary of Estimated Costs of the Procedures

The procedures described in this study, especially the client outcome monitoring procedures, are complex. There are numerous tasks to be done and numerous difficult questions to be resolved. The client outcome monitoring procedures are likely to cost a state government at least $50,000 to $100,000 annually for a sample of 2,000 to 3,000 clients. (Actual out-of-pocket costs will depend on the extent to which existing government personnel can be utilized.) The cost of a statewide citizen survey on the unmet needs of 1,500-2,000 households will range from $25,000 to $50,000 annually unless it is part of a multi-service citizen survey and costs are shared with other state agencies.

There will be a great temptation for states (and local governments) to simplify and cut corners. As usual, the trade-offs among cost, reliability, and validity have to be closely examined. Some simplifications clearly warrant exploration. These include the use of a combination of mail, telephone, and in-person interviews to reduce follow-up interview costs, an initial focus on a smaller number of goals (perhaps Title XX Goals I, II, and III), and somewhat smaller sample sizes. But it should also be pointed out that "you get what you pay for." Many kinds of simplification (some of which are

EXHIBIT 2

ILLUSTRATIVE FORMAT FOR SOCIAL SERVICES CLIENT OUTCOME FINDINGS:
CLIENT CONDITION OR CATEGORY AT ENTRY, BY GEOGRAPHICAL REGION

Client Condition or Category at Entry[b]	Total			Region I[a]			Region II			Region III		
	Percentage			Percentage			Percentage			Percentage		
	Improved[c]	Same	Worsened[c]	Improved	Same	Worsened	Improved	Same	Worsened	Improved	Same	Worsened
Category 1.												
Category 2.												
Category 3.												
Category 4.												
Category 5.												
TOTAL												

a. Various types of geographical subdivisions could be used here. North Carolina, for example, has four administrative regions for social services. Groups of counties are another possibility.

b. These could be "severity of problem" categories or demographic characteristic categories, for example, various age groups, types of problems, and the like. Each such type of categorization could, by itself, by the subject of a separate table.

c. "Improved" and "worsened" need to be defined specifically in terms of the items in the data collection instruments.

discussed in this report) can quickly weaken the quality of the information. If a government wants meaningful outcome information, it should avoid excessive skimping on efforts to achieve it. The cost of evaluation even with these procedures is likely to be only a small percentage of the total cost of social service programs and, if used properly, can potentially pay for itself several times over.

Future Research Steps

Much remains to be done in order to develop satisfactory outcome monitoring procedures. Future research should probably include the following:

-Further development and testing of this and other versions of the data collection instrument for client outcomes to make it as appropriate and comprehensive as possible for varying client groups and social services. In addition, scoring procedures need to be developed and tested.

-Validation of the questionnaire so that user states can feel more confident about the ability of the questionnaire to elicit, without major bias, the information desired.

-Further exploration of the sampling issues discussed in Chapter 3. The choice of sampling procedures, sample size, timing of intake and follow-up interviews, and interviewing technique are some of the issues that can best be determined through further testing.

-Considerable further development of procedures for the assessment of "appropriateness of care."

-Examination of ways to maximize the utility of client outcome data. Formats and analyses need to be spelled out and illustrated in greater detail.

-Examination of the use of statewide surveys for estimating "unmet need" for social services, in order to better determine the surveys' validity and utility.

-Examination of the costs involved in outcome monitoring.

Future research efforts should be conducted with the help and advice of county-level agencies. These are likely to be among those most interested in the findings. They will also be of major importance in making the procedures more practical, as well as themselves being potentially major users of such procedures.

Chapter 1

CLIENT OUTCOME INFORMATION TO BE OBTAINED

This chapter, along with Chapters 2 through 4, provides preliminary suggestions for procedures that agencies can use to monitor client outcomes of social services.[1] Efforts hitherto conducted by state, county, and private social service agencies have tended to be one-time-only studies or endeavors that focused on one service or one goal.

The focus of this effort is on developing procedures that can be undertaken on a regular basis, say annually, in order to provide government officials with regular outcome information for detecting changes and time trends. The focus is on the client and on the client's array of problems, whether or not the client receives more than one service. Thus, although the outcome data can be analyzed to derive some findings on specific services, the focus here is on estimating the extent to which the client's problems improved after receiving services.[2]

This chapter presents the rationale for the first ten of the dimensions listed in the Summary (Exhibit 1), and for the various items of information suggested to assess each.[3] Preliminary versions of specific question wordings are suggested. The sources from which the questions have been adapted are indicated, along with references to alternative sets of questions when appropriate.

---

1. Efficiency measures and cost criteria, although important for many management purposes, are not discussed in this report. However, efficiency measures need to consider the quality of output obtained. Thus outcome measurement procedures such as those discussed here are likely to be essential for determining whether greater efficiency represents true improvement of merely reduction in cost at the expense of quality.

2. Other similar efforts that have recently been initiated include those of the Northwest Federation of States (and its test in Montana) and the West Virginia-Case Western Reserve study. Volume II contains a discussion of these and other approaches.

3. The "appropriateness of care" dimension is discussed in Chapter 2; the "unmet need" dimension is discussed in Chapter 5. The preliminary questionnaire to collect most of the outcome data is presented in its entirety in Appendix A.

The monitoring procedure would begin with the drawing of a sample of clients coming into the social service system (see Chapter 3). For those clients consenting to participation in the study, basic information would be obtained, including type of problem(s), age group, sex, race, and social services (type and length) provided to the client. The addresses and telephone numbers of the clients and others who might help locate the clients at the time of follow-up would also be obtained. This basic information would be obtained either from clients directly or from government records and would be entered on standard forms for use by interviewers as well as for use in subsequently locating clients for follow-up interviews and for tabulating outcomes according to client characteristics. The interviewers would not see the clients' case files.

Interviewers would administer questionnaires to each client in the sample at intake and at follow-up. Even though a client may have sought social services to obtain help with a problem involving only one dimension, it is suggested that the entire questionnaire be administered to each client except for dimensions which are clearly inappropriate. (Chapter 2 provides suggestions on which dimensions to use for various client groups.)

Administering the entire questionnaire will provide a comprehensive perspective on the client that is useful, especially in the frequent situations where clients have multiple problems. It will also permit assessment of side-effects, both beneficial and harmful, arising from social services. Administering the entire instrument, however, also has drawbacks. It adds to the length of interviews, and it may on occasion confuse the interpretation of changes effected by social services. A client may have one problem at entry, for example, and a completely different one at the time of follow-up.

Need to Classify Clients by "Difficulty"

Information on client status at intake would be obtained not only as a baseline for measuring changes but also for classifying clients by degree of "difficulty." This classification allows more meaningful comparisons, since differences in client mix can be identified. A hypothetical illustration will help to explain this.

Suppose the findings for two different client samples from two periods of time (or from two separate facilities) were the following:

	Total Cases	Number and Percentage of Cases Where Dependency Was Reduced
High Client Difficulty	400	100 (25%)
Low Client Difficulty	100	100 (100%)
Total, Sample 1	500	200 (40%)
High Client Difficulty	100	0 (0%)
Low Client Difficulty	400	300 (75%)
Total, Sample 2	500	300 (60%)

Based on the totals alone, the results for the second sample appear superior, because success was achieved in 60 percent of the cases. Sample 1, however, shows a much higher success rate for both "high difficulty" clients (25 percent as compared to 0 percent for sample 2) and for "low difficulty" clients (100 percent as compared to 75 percent for sample 2). The overall higher success rate for the second sample stemmed from its having a larger proportion of clients with low difficulty.[1]

Time Period Covered by the Questions

In most cases, the questions illustrated below (and in Appendix A) ask about specific conditions over a specific time period, such as the preceding month, rather than asking clients only about their current situation. The latter would be likely to encourage clients to overemphasize very recent events, that is, those of the previous day or two; clients might tend to focus on what might be unusual or temporary situations. On the other hand, questions involving longer time periods, such as three or six months, would put a larger burden on respondents' memories. The one-month period chosen for most of the questions is judgmental and not based on empirical data. Other periods are used when circumstances seem to require them--for example, for employment history.

Criteria Used for Identifying Conditions To Be Monitored

We have used, somewhat loosely, three general criteria to help identify conditions which should be included. Each condition to be monitored should shed direct light on one of the following questions:

1. Is the person functioning adequately in "society"?
2. Is the person "hurting"?[2]
3. Is the person engaging in antisocial (i.e., illegal) behavior?

The following sections discuss each of the ten dimensions of client outcomes, the conditions we have identified as being associated with each, and the specific questions for obtaining the information.

A Note on Questionnaire Validity

The questions discussed in this chapter have not, for the most part, been subjected to any extensive validation efforts. Some pretesting has been undertaken by the North Carolina-Urban Institute team; approximately forty interviews of clients in two North Carolina counties were undertaken, and some modifications were subsequently made.

---

1. There appear to be few current uses of categorization of clients by degree of difficulty other than in vocational rehabilitation programs. More typically, clients are classified only by type of problem.

2. A client's self-perception of "hurting" appears important in addition to more "objective" indications of client condition.

Full-scale validation efforts cannot be undertaken by a state until specific decisions are made as to when, where, and how the questionnaire is to be administered. These questions are discussed in Chapters 3 and 4. The set of questions in this chapter is presented as a starting point for governments in identifying the information necessary for monitoring client outcomes.

Economic Self-Support

The indicators and questions for this dimension are presented in Table 1. The outcomes of services aimed at economic self-support are expressed in terms of getting a job, keeping it for some period of time, actual earnings, and extent of dependence upon public assistance. These indicate changes in the degree of dependency; that is, progress toward, even if not achievement of, the goal of economic self-support. Change in the "employability level" of the respondent is not here considered as an outcome; it is, however, an intermediate objective for social services and some jurisdictions may want to include an indicator for changes in employability.[1] "Employability level" at intake would also be useful for classifying clients by difficulty.

Employment history should be sought for a period of time (a three-month period is suggested here) because it seems that a more meaningful indicator of improvement would thus be obtained than if the questions were limited to employment status at the time of the interview. Even a three-month period may pose a problem, since employment may vary seasonally. Some clients, for example, may always be more likely to have a job in the summer than in the fall, regardless of services provided. Part of this problem is mitigated if the follow-up interview is conducted, as suggested, 12 months after intake; the three-month period of assessment will, in such cases, cover the same season and hence will at least improve the comparability of the before-versus-after assessments.

The questions presented, although not taken from any one source, are fairly commonly used in various surveys.

Ability to Undertake Activities of Daily Living

The ability to perform the activities of daily living is sometimes used as a substitute for "self-sufficiency"; however, there are varying interpretations of what it means to be "self-sufficient." At one extreme, it includes conditions that make for a contented, fulfilled adult; at the other, it implies merely the ability to undertake the most basic activities of daily living. The latter seems too narrow a definition of self-sufficiency, while the former cannot readily be defined clearly enough to be operational. An intermediate position seems appropriate; hence the ability to undertake the activities of daily living is considered as one aspect among others of self-sufficiency.

Ordinary, day-to-day activities can be divided into (1) basic personal activities such as bathing, dressing, and eating, and (2) activities that one has to perform (or have done) in our society in order to live a normal life--labeled by some researchers "instrumental activities." Personal and instrumental activities are combined in Indicator 6 of Exhibit 1. Making a

---

1. There are several data collection instruments available to assess employability.

TABLE 1: ECONOMIC SELF-SUPPORT
(RELATED PRIMARILY TO GOAL 1)

INDICATOR	QUESTION	COMMENT
1. Current employ-ment status	1. What is your main activity now?	
2. Length of time employed in three-month period prior to interview	2. Approximately how many months/weeks of the past three months were you employed?	This is based on the assumption that "steadiness of employment" is an outcome that social services would want to affect.
3. Quality of jobs held	3. In the past three months, during the time you were working, what kinds of jobs did you have?	This question, along with question 4, provides an employment profile for the three-month period preceding the interview. The assumption is that quality of jobs, amount of time working, and earnings are all outcomes pertaining to self-support. The responses to this question might be coded as, for example, unskilled labor, skilled labor, professional and technical labor. (Another perspective would be obtained by asking respondents about their job satisfaction level.)
4. Amount earned in three-month period prior to interview	4. For each job you mentioned above, (a) how long did you work at the job, (b) was it part-time or full-time, and (c) how much did you get paid?	This question, detailed as it is, is more likely to elicit an accurate response than a general question that asks about earnings in each of the three months. It seems preferable to ask about overall pay rather than "take-home pay," since the former can be compared to federally determined poverty levels for gauging whether "self-support" has been achieved. However, it is possible that respondents may find it easier to give information on "take-home pay."
5. Extent of depen-dence on public assistance	5. During the past three months, did you or any other member of your family receive any money from the following? About how much? Who received it? --Unemployment compensation or workmen's compensation --Welfare payments, aid to dependent children --Food stamps --Salaries, pensions, and other private means of support --Other (specify)	The intention is to calculate the extent of public assistance as a percentage of some norm, such as the poverty level. One issue is whether such services as Medicaid, transportation services, meals-on-wheels, etc., should be included. The problem is that it is difficult to estimate the cost of such services. Even food stamps involve an exchange of money for greater values in food. This question is also intended to be useful for cases in which economic self-support is not the primary goal. For example, when a child is placed in a foster home, the economic well-being of the family may be considered to be part of a "good" placement. Hence, the question asks about the income of the entire family, from all sources, not only public assistance.

distinction between these two sets of activities is useful, however, because
it will make sense in some cases (for example, for children aged ten or so)
to ask about a client's personal activities and omit the instrumental
activities. (Ten-year-olds can be expected to perform self-care activities,
but in this society they are not expected to cook and clean house for
themselves.)

"Personal" Activities of Daily Living. The first half of Table 2 presents
the indicators and questions that relate to clients' ability to care for their
own person--eating, dressing, bathing, personal grooming, toileting, and walking.

The questions included here have been adapted primarily from the Duke
University Older Americans Resources and Services Program (OARS) Multidimensional Functional Assessment Questionnaire.[1] Other sources included the Katz
Activities of Daily Living Index,[2] the Barthel Index,[3] and the HEW Classification.[4] These sources call for the ratings to be made by clinicians, except
for the Duke University procedures, which used trained interviewers. The use
of clinicians, including caseworkers, is difficult and costly. Therefore,
the questions presented here have been modified to facilitate direct administration to clients by trained interviewers who do not need to have a clinical
background.

"Instrumental" Activities of Daily Living. The ability to perform activities instrumental to living in society is part of a "minimal" definition
of self-sufficiency. The second group of questions in Table 2 have been adapted, for direct administration by trained interviewers, from the Lawton-Brody
Instrumental Activities of Daily Living scale[5] and the Duke University OARS
scale.[6] There are questions on meal preparation, doing housework, telephoning,
shopping, doing laundry, and traveling beyond walking distance.

Physical Health

Social services do not include the actual provision of medical services.
Some social service agencies, however, assist clients in obtaining medical

1. Duke University Center for the Study of Aging and Human Development,
Older Americans Resources and Services Program, "OARS Multidimensional Functional
Assessment Questionnaire" (Durham, N.C., April 1975).

2. Sidney Katz et al., "Studies of Illness in the Aged, The Index of ADL:
A Standardized Measure of Biological and Psychosocial Function," Journal of
the American Medical Association 185, no. 12 (September 21, 1963):914-19.

3. Florence I. Mahoney and Dorothea W. Barthel, "Functional Evaluation:
The Barthel Index," Maryland State Medical Journal, February 1965.

4. U.S. Department of Health, Education and Welfare, Patient Classification
for Long-Term Care: User's Manual, by Ellen W. Jones (Washington, D.C.: DHEW
pub. no. HRA74-3107, December 1973).

5. M. Powell Lawton and Elaine M. Brody, "Assessment of Older People:
Self-Maintaining and Instrumental Activities of Daily Living," The Gerontologist
9, no. 3 (Autumn 1969):179-86.

6. Duke University, "OARS Multidimensional Functional Assessment Questionnaire."

TABLE 2: ABILITY TO UNDERTAKE ACTIVITIES OF
DAILY LIVING (PRIMARILY USEFUL FOR GOAL 2)

INDICATOR	QUESTION	COMMENT
6. Level of functioning on activities of daily living	In the past month, did someone help you 6. --feed yourself? 7. --dress and undress yourself? 8. --take a bath or shower? 9. --use the bathroom? 10. --take care of your appearance? IF "YES" a. How did this person help you? b. If you didn't have someone to help you, would you have been able to do it? d. Have you needed any special devices? IF "NO" c. Do you feel that you needed help? d. Have you needed any special devices? 11. Can you --walk a mile or more without help of any kind? --walk a mile or more without any help but with some difficulty? --walk or transport yourself for a mile or more with adaptive devices? --walk or transport yourself for a mile or more but only with someone else along? --move around the house with help from another person? --sit alone and propel wheelchair around the house but need help getting into and out of the wheelchair? --Do you need to have the wheelchair pushed by someone? --Are you bedfast? In the past month, did someone help you 12. --prepare meals? 13. --do housework? 14. --use the telephone? 15. --go shopping for routine things like groceries or clothes? 16. --do your laundry? 17. --take your medicine? IF "YES" a. How did this person help you? b. If you didn't have someone to help you, would you have been able to do it? IF "NO" c. Do you feel that you needed help? 18. In the past month, have you been able to get to places beyond walking distance --without help? --with help of special devices? --with some help? --with considerable help? --not without special arrangements?	These questions are aimed at assessing the ability of the person to perform various activities, that is, whether the person can perform them without assistance, with the help of devices, with help from another person, or not at all. [a] These questions are aimed at assessing the ability of the person to perform various activities, that is, whether the person can perform them without assistance, with help from another person, or not at all. The "b" part of each question is included to identify those situations in which a person does not, for instance, do the cooking because of societal or family "roles" but has the ability to do it. It differentiates between physical ability to perform an activity and unwillingness to do it or lack of experience in doing it. (The interviewer has to be trained to probe on "b" in order to make sure it is ability which is being assessed.)

a. "Continence" is not included here. Questions on continence were not generally included in the sources used to develop these questions. However, there are indications that questions on continence are useful in identifying those needing nursing home care. The addition of such questions should be considered for future versions of the questionnaire.

services. If one accepts the premise that a person's problems often affect physical health, then physical health status becomes, at least indirectly, an "outcome" of social services. It should be noted that physical health, probably more than other client conditions, is likely to be affected by external factors unrelated to the provision of social services.

One way of assessing a person's health is to ask about the existence of medical disorders, physical problems, medications taken, and so on, but we were not able to find a satisfactory set of questions and procedures that elicits such information and then aggregates the responses into a meaningful "estimate" of a person's physical health status.

Instead, the series of questions presented in Table 3 focuses on the extent to which the health of clients affects "functioning" and clients' perception of their overall "healthiness." While the previous sets of questions on activities of daily living seek information on the functional limitations of those who are chronically disabled as well as those who are acutely ill, the "physical health" questions focus on "sickness."

The questions on number of days of restricted activity are patterned after questions in the Health Interview Survey of the National Center for Health Statistics. The death of a client between intake and follow-up should be recorded as part of the assessment (Item R-1, in Appendix A).

Mental Distress

Mental illness is sometimes one of the client's problems. It can affect and be affected by the client's social situation and functioning. Hence, "mental health" seems generally accepted as an outcome relevant to social services. But how can "mental health" be validly assessed? What should be included under "mental health"?

A wide variety of behavioral and attitudinal conditions can be construed as part of mental health. In selecting conditions to assess, such concepts as "self-image," "self-esteem," "mood," and "defensiveness" were omitted, because these are abstract and their relationship to functioning is difficult to interpret. Such conditions as nervousness, headaches, and indigestion seem more relevant to outcome-monitoring purposes. These conditions seem to be more directly related to a person's functioning, more indicative of a client's degree of "hurting," and simpler to define and measure than the less concrete concepts listed above. (Jurisdictions that consider such client characteristics as "self-image" to be direct indicators of the degree to which a client is "hurting" may want to add appropriate questions to attempt to obtain the requisite information.)

The first ten questions from the Denver Community Mental Health Questionnaire have been included in the recommended procedures for measuring mental distress (see Table 4). This short and easily administered set of

TABLE 3: PHYSICAL HEALTH (PRIMARILY FOR GOAL 2)

INDICATOR	QUESTION	COMMENT
7. Number of days of restricted activity during the past three months	19. During the past three months, how many days were you so sick that you were unable to carry on your usual activities--such as going to work or working around the house?	Responses may include days lost because of emotional problems, but inasmuch as this is manifested as "sickness," it seems to be a valid inclusion. Item R-1 (see Appendix A) is needed to identify those cases in which the client has died during the interval between the intake and follow-up interviews.
	20. Did you go to the hospital anytime as an in-patient in the past three months? For how many days?	Information on out-patient days and visits to a doctor or clinic are excluded on the assumption that in-patient days indicate not only a more serious problem but also "functioning" days lost.
8. Overall health as perceived by the client	21. How would you rate your overall health in the past three months--good, fair, or poor?	Is the client "hurting" as perceived by the client? This provides another perspective on the person's health over and above the functioning aspects.
	22. In the past three months, how much have your health troubles stood in the way of your doing the things you wanted to do--not at all, a little (some), a great deal?	
9. Client's perception of degree of improvement since receiving services	23. (FOR FOLLOW-UP ONLY) When you compare your health now to what it was like before you started receiving help from (name of agency), would you say it is now much better, somewhat better, about the same, somewhat worse?	This follow-up question has been included both for validation purposes and for recording client perceptions of "change."

TABLE 4: MENTAL DISTRESS (PRIMARILY RELATED TO GOAL 2)

INDICATOR	QUESTION	COMMENT
10. Index of mental distress	In the past month, how often have you felt 24. --fearful or afraid? 25. --sad or depressed? 26. --angry? 27. --mixed up or confused? 28. --tense or uptight? 29. --trouble with sleeping? 30. --trouble with headaches? 31. --trouble with poor appetite? 32. --trouble with upset stomach? 33. --very tired? --never (0) --once or twice (1) --often (2) --almost always (3)	These questions individually may not seem to be indicative of psychological distress (for example, one can suffer from indigestion or headaches because of frequent parties), and at some time or another most people suffer from these symptoms. As a group, however, there is some validity to the claim that they indicate "psychological distress." Note that this group of questions has been subjected to more validation tests than have the others. The questions are not intended for individual scoring but are to be interpreted only as a group. Some people may feel that persons answering will tend to be unduly influenced by very recent circumstances. The assumption here is that, except in unusual situations, persons who are generally "healthy" are not likely to score very high on the scale. The scoring for the set is done by adding up values for each response category (see the numbers in parentheses). Each question is assumed to have equal weight. This means that a response of "almost always" has three times the value of a response of "once or twice."
11. Indication of major mental depression	34. In the past month, how often have you felt you can't cope with things--never, once or twice, often, or almost always? 35. In the past month, have you ever been so upset that someone had to come in and take care of you? For how many days? 36. In the past month, how often did you feel you did not want to go on living--never, once or twice, often, or almost always?	These three questions explore to a further degree the "mental distress" assessed by the first ten questions. A person can indicate a high amount of psychological distress on the Denver questions and yet not experience a total inability to cope. Inability to cope, or to function, suicidal feelings, and the like, are more serious manifestations of "psychological distress" than are the Denver questions. So also are the occurrence of suicides and nervous breakdowns--items R-2 and R-3 of Appendix A, to be obtained from records.
12. Degree of loneliness/ isolation	37. In the past month, did you have as much contact as you would like with a person(s) that you felt close to--somebody that you could trust and confide in? 38. In the past month, did you see your relatives and friends as often as you wanted to, or were you somewhat unhappy about how little you saw them, or were you considerably unhappy about how little you saw them?	These questions are most appropriate for those for whom obtaining social companionship is most likely to be a problem because of physical infirmity (for example, respondents who are blind, handicapped, elderly, or shut-ins). A single question on "loneliness" (see question 39) might be sufficient, but pride or other factors may sometimes prevent respondents from admitting that they are lonely. Hence the inclusion of questions 37 and 38 is intended to assess whether they are seeing people and experiencing close relationships as much as they would like. Others have included questions on the actual (rather than perceived) contact--for example, "How often do you talk on the telephone a week--
	(continued)	(continued)

TABLE 4, CONTINUED

INDICATOR	QUESTION	COMMENT
Degree of loneliness/ isolation (continued)	39. Over the past month, did you find yourself feeling quite lonely--almost never, sometimes, often, almost always, or don't know?	once a day or more, 2-6 times per week, once, or not at all?"[a] Such a question provides "objective" information on number of contacts. Nonetheless, without some accepted norm or criterion for determining the "loneliness" threshold, such information can yield highly ambiguous results. The questions as given here are also likely to elicit varying definitions of "as much contact as you would like," "as often as you want to," and so forth, but the rating will be anchored on the respondents' own perception of "loneliness" and therefore represent the degree to which respondents are "hurting."
13. Overall attitude toward life in general	40. Taking everything into consideration, how would you describe your satisfaction with life in general at the present time--good, fair, not sure, or poor?	A general question that is commonly used. It has been used both by the Duke University study[b] and by the Florida study (although both were for older citizens).
14. Client's perception of degree of improvement since receiving services	41. (FOR FOLLOW-UP ONLY) Since you started getting help from (name of agency), are your problems much better, somewhat better, the same, somewhat worse, or much worse?	This question should also provide at least a rough validation of the change scores for other parts of this dimension for each respondent. In the opinion of some members of the North Carolina advisory committee, the phrase "since receiving social services" could easily be mistaken for "since receiving Social Security." Since clients often receive services from more than one agency, the issue becomes one of identifying "social services." The name or location of the building in which county social services are located is one possibility; however, in some counties, the same building may house other government services as well.

a. Florida Department of Health and Rehabilitative Services, Assessment of Needs of Low-Income, Urban Elderly Persons in the Florida Counties of Dade, Pinellas and Palm Beach (May 1973).

b. Duke University, "OARS Multidimensional Functional Assessment Questionnaire."

questions attempts to assess symptoms that contribute to "mental distress."[1]
It is important to note that these ten questions (questions 24-33 in Appendix
A), which comprise the mental distress indicator, are not intended to be
scored and displayed individually. One score is to be calculated for the
set and that score provided to users. Any individual can, on occasion, display one or more of the individual symptoms. The discriminating ability of
the scale derives from collective consideration of the responses to all the
questions. The Denver team has conducted several tests of the scale's
validity and reliability that indicate its ability to discriminate between
mental health program clients and the general population.[2]

The Denver questions ask the client about "the last couple of days."
For the purposes of this work, it was felt that a person's state of mind
during such a short time was not sufficiently meaningful; hence, the time
reference has been changed to ask about the month immediately preceding the
interview. In addition, the words "indigestion" and "fatigue" in the Denver
questionnaire were changed to "upset stomach" and "feeling very tired," since
the North Carolina pretest showed the former terms to be more difficult for
respondents to understand.[3]

There are a number of other mental health scales available, but the
brevity of the Denver scale, in the absence of evidence that these other scales
provide substantially superior data, appears to leave the Denver scale with an
advantage over the others. Some alternatives are the Symptom-90 Checklist,[4]

1. James A. Ciarlo and Jacqueline Reihman, "The Denver Community Mental
Health Questionnaire: Development of a Multi-Dimensional Program Evaluation
Instrument" (Denver, Colo.: Mental Health Systems Evaluation Project of the
Northwest Denver Mental Health Center and the University of Denver, 1974).
This questionnaire has been used primarily to measure the functioning level
of different samples of clients at successive time intervals; it has not yet
been used to compare "before and after" readings on the same clients or even
the same group of clients. Nonetheless, there seems to be no reason why it
cannot be used to assess "change" scores for the same sets of clients.

2. The team compared (1) scores obtained from clients with those based on
interviewer judgments (the correlation coefficient was 0.94 for a sample size
of 349); (2) scores obtained from clients with ratings made by persons who knew
the clients well (the correlation coefficient was 0.59 for N=91); (3) client
scores with global ratings made by clinicians (the correlation coefficient was
0.35 for N=71); and (4) client scores with scores obtained from a sample of
Denver residents. The standardized scores for the psychological distress com-
ponent were 50.0 for the community (N=90) and 44.4 for the clients (N=538).
Higher scores indicate better functioning. The Denver scale was found to differentiate between the two sets of respondents. See also David C. Speer, "An
Evaluation of the Denver Community Mental Health Questionnaire as a Measure of
Outpatient Treatment Effectiveness" (Columbus, Ind.: Quinco Consulting Center,
1976).

3. Even these "minor" changes could affect the validity results of the
Denver team. Pending more testing, it would appear that the changes would not
adversely affect validity, and might even increase it.

4. Leonard R. Derogatis, Ronald S. Lipman, and Lino Covi, "SCL-90: An
Outpatient Psychiatric Rating Scale--Preliminary Report," Psychopharmacology
Bulletin 9 (1973):13-28. Leonard R. Derogatis et al., "The Hopkins Symptom
Checklist (HSCL): A Self-Report Symptom Inventory," Behavioral Science 19,
no. 1 (January 1974):1-15.

the Midtown Manhattan Mental Health Questionnaire,[1] and the Health Opinion Survey.[2] The Symptom-90 Checklist is easy to understand and administer and deals with a large variety of distress "symptoms"; however, it contains ninety items. The Midtown Manhattan Mental Health Questionnaire, with twenty-two items, has been administered to the general community to estimate the incidence of mental health problem. It is somewhat longer than the Denver questionnaire; however, one study found that a set of nine items in the Manhattan scale provided results similar to those obtained by using all twenty-two items.[3]

In addition to this set of questions, Table 4 contains questions intended to obtain four other perspectives on mental condition. Questions 34-36, along with items R-2 and R-3 (incidents of nervous breakdowns and attempted suicides), provide an indication of the existence of major mental health problems. Questions 37-39 attempt to provide an indication of the extent of loneliness/isolation experienced by the client, a subject often raised in social services research and one not explicitly covered by the other questions. Question 40 provides an overall rating from clients on their satisfaction with life in general. Question 41 queries clients as to their own perception of the extent to which their problems have improved (or worsened) since receiving services.

Alcohol and Drug Abuse

Alcohol and drug abuse are two kinds of behavior that tend to be related to social maladjustment. Where they exist with clients, they are generally accepted as conditions to be alleviated. Table 5 presents the questions that attempt to assess problems related to alcohol and drug abuse. An important issue here is honesty of response from clients. Clients may withhold or distort information. Thus, unless clients are admitted alcoholics or drug addicts, it may be difficult to determine the existence of alcohol or drug abuse either at intake or at follow-up.

To identify alcohol problems, six questions are included (questions 42-47), three of which (43-45) were obtained by combining seven questions from the Denver Community Mental Health Questionnaire. The Denver questions on alcohol abuse have shown some ability to differentiate between the community at large and clients of community mental health centers. It is possible, however, that persons seeking mental health services are more likely to admit alcohol abuse than are clients for social services. (For example, a client receiving protective services may be reluctant to admit to alcoholism.) The questions shown

1. T.S. Langner, "A Twenty-Two Item Screening Score of Psychiatric Symptoms Indicating Impairment," Journal of Health and Human Behavior 3 (1962): 269-76. L. Srole et al., Mental Health in the Metropolis: The Midtown Manhattan Study, vol. 1 (New York: McGraw-Hill, 1962).

2. Dorothea C. Leighton et al., The Character of Danger: Psychiatric Symptoms in Selected Communities (New York: Basic Books, 1963). Allister M. Macmillan, "The Health Opinion Survey: Technique for Estimating Prevalence of Psychoneurotic and Related Types of Disorder in Communities," Psychological Reports 3, supp. 7 (1957).

3. Jerome G. Manis et al., "Validating a Mental Health Scale," American Sociological Review 28, no. 1 (February 1963):108-16.

TABLE 5: ALCOHOL AND DRUG ABUSE
(PRIMARILY FOR GOAL 2)

INDICATOR	QUESTION	COMMENT
15. Extent of alcohol abuse	42. In the past month, about how often did you drink alcohol? --almost never (no drinking at all or less than one drink per week) --occasionally (up to three drinks per week, but no more) --often (four or more drinks per week)	The response categories for question 42 have been obtained from the New Jersey needs survey.[a] The focus of this set of questions is not on measuring the frequency of intake but the extent of problems caused by alcohol intake. Question 42 is mainly an introduction to the next three questions.
	43. Has your drinking caused any difficulties or problems for you in your emotional or physical health in the past month? 44. Has your drinking caused any problems with your employer or job in the past month?	Questions 43-45 are adapted from questions in the Denver Community Mental Health Questionnaire. We have combined its questions in order to cut down the total number. The words "problem" and "difficulties" are somewhat general, but any effort to pinpoint them would result in the addition of several questions, and brevity is a virtue, at least for this questionnaire. The response categories (never, sometimes, . . .) are somewhat vague and should be defined more clearly.
	45. Has your drinking caused any difficulties or problems with your family or your friends in the past month?	The Denver questionnaire separates question 45 into a question regarding problems with spouse, another on problems with children, and a third on problems with friends.
	46. In the past month, have you been arrested for public drunkenness or drinking-related charges? How many times?	For active clients, this information may be in case records (see R-4). The information for R-4 (and R-5 for drug abuse) would be obtained from records (or if the client is found to be in jail for such an incident when the interviewer locates the client for follow-up). Inspection of police records is not recommended--see text.
	47. Do you feel you have an alcohol problem? IF "YES" Are you getting any help for the problem?	This question provides another opportunity for the respondent to indicate the existence of a drinking problem.
	R-4. Evidence of at least one arrest or conviction related to use of alcohol during past three months	
16. Extent of drug abuse	48. In the past month, did you use drugs of any kind other than alcohol? Which drugs did you use, and how often--heroin, morphine, cocaine, amphetamines, barbiturates, other (specify)?[b] (continued)	Marijuana usage is such a controversial issue that we suggest it be excluded. However, some may want to include it. It may be useful to include the question, "Are you using the drug(s) on the prescription of a doctor?" if the state decides that prescribed drugs do not constitute "drug abuse." (continued)

a. The New Jersey social services needs assessment questionnaire, RL Associates (April 1976); see Volume II for details.

b. The response categories for this question have been taken from Louis H. Blair and John Sessler, Drug Program Assessment (Washington, D.C.: The Drug Abuse Council, February 1974), p. 49.

TABLE 5, CONTINUED

INDICATOR	QUESTION	COMMENT
Extent of drug abuse (continued)	49. Has your use of drugs caused you any problems in your emotional or physical health in the past month?	Questions 49-51 are adapted from questions in the Denver Community Mental Health Questionnaire. We have combined its questions to cut down the total number. The response categories (never, sometimes, . . .) need to be defined more clearly.
	50. Has your use of drugs caused any problems with your employer or job in the past month?	
	51. Has your use of drugs caused any problems with your family or friends in the past month?	
	52. In the past month, have you been arrested for illegal possession or use of drugs? How many times?	For active clients, this information may be obtainable from case records.
	53. Do you feel you have a drug problem? IF "YES" Are you getting any help for the problem?	This question provides another opportunity for the respondent to indicate the existence of a drug problem.
	R-5. Evidence of at least one arrest or conviction re- lated to use of drugs during past three months	

here therefore need testing; there is no guarantee that they can unearth hidden alcoholics.

An alternative set of questions is the so-called "CAGE" questionnaire, designed to uncover "hidden alcoholics."[1] Assuming that clients will take great care to hide alcoholism, Ewing and Rouse developed a questionnaire to identify alcoholism, defined as "the physical, mental, or social incapacity produced by prolonged, excessive drinking." Four questions were selected as those that best screened out alcoholics. The four "CAGE" questions are:

1. Have you ever felt you ought to Cut down on your drinking?
2. Have people Annoyed you by criticizing your drinking?
3. Have you ever felt bad or Guilty about your drinking?
4. Have you ever had a drink first thing in the morning to steady your nerves or to get rid of a hangover? ("Eye-opener")

The researchers suggest that three positive replies indicate possible alcoholism, and that even two are cause for suspicion. When the responses of patients in an alcoholic rehabilitation center were compared with those of a set of nonalcoholic patients, the results showed that the questions were able to produce answers that differentiated between alcoholics and nonalcoholics.[2] (Surprisingly, the sensitivity of the questions is apparently greater if a two- or three-item positive response is taken as the criterion for indicating alcoholism.[3]) These questions, moreover, did not seem to arouse indignation in respondents.

Although the CAGE questionnaire is a good means of identifying alcoholics, it was not developed as a way of assessing changes in degree of alcohol abuse. But there seems to be no reason why it could not indicate a change within the past several months from the status of alcoholic to that of nonalcoholic, especially if the wording was altered to ask only about the past, say, month. The questions, however, may not be sensitive to changes of lesser magnitude, such as a reduction in quantity imbibed. However, if it is true that an alcoholic cannot reduce the amount of alcohol consumed, so that the only options are to remain an alcoholic or practice total abstinence and only this extreme condition is of concern to the social service agency, the CAGE questions might be an appropriate change indicator.

---

1. J. Ewing and B. Rouse, "Identifying the 'Hidden Alcoholic,'" paper presented at the 29th International Congress on Alcohol and Drug Dependence, Sydney, Australia, February 2-6, 1970, p. 3.

2. Ibid., pp. 13, 14, and 15.

3. Demmie Mayfield, Gail McLeod, and Patricia Hall, "The CAGE Questionnaire: Validation of a New Alcoholism Screening Instrument," American Journal of Psychiatry 131, no. 10 (October 1974):1121-23. Alcoholics are more likely to be identified if the following criterion for responses is used: "positive responses to 2 or 3 questions, rather than positive responses to 4 questions." Apparently, question 2 was not so good a predictor in this study; 50 percent of the alcoholics failed to give a positive response to that question.

The next set of questions in Table 5 (questions 48-53) deals with drug abuse. Honesty of response is perhaps even more a concern here than in the case of alcohol abuse. The following are some of the advantages and disadvantages of different procedures to obtain information on drug abuse:[1]

--Asking the client directly (as called for in questions 48-53). Unless the client has a police record of drug usage and is aware that the interviewer knows about the record, the client may not admit to drug usage.

--Obtaining information from the police department. If there is good cooperation between the police department and the social services agency at the county level, some identification of drug users from police records is possible, but this is generally unlikely. Moreover, use of police department records may constitute "invasion of privacy" of the client.

--Asking someone close to the client. The questions on drug abuse can be adapted slightly and administered by an interviewer to a friend or a relative of the client if the client has given permission. However, this raises two problems: First, it is likely that only a close relative or friend will be able to give accurate information about drug or alcohol usage, but few interviews of relatives or friends are likely to be possible because most clients do not want anyone else brought into the matter.[2] In most cases, the explicit permission of the client to interview other persons must be obtained. Second, friends or relatives being interviewed may answer in a way that they believe advantageous to the client, such as giving an answer which the friend or relative thinks is likely to increase the client's chances of receiving state assistance.

The questions included in Table 5 to identify drug problems have wording similar to that used for alcohol problems. Three of the drug questions (49-51) were obtained by combining seven of the questions in the Denver questionnaire.

It is clear that considerably more testing is needed on the alcohol and drug abuse questions before they can be used with confidence. Although all the dimensions have validity problems, the questions dealing with this dimension appear to have significantly less face credibility than do the others.

Information on other types of antisocial behavior, such as vandalism, destructiveness, aggression against others, and other criminal acts related

---

1. The Drug Abuse Council (Washington, D.C.) did not recommend any interview procedures to assess extent of drug abuse. There are some medical tests, like urine testing, to determine drug usage, but these do not seem suitable for use here.

2. Only in cases of severely mentally retarded, senile, or other such clients can one make the assumption that interviews of relatives or friends are both appropriate and feasible.

to alcohol or drug abuse, is also relevant. For example, information that
the client has been arrested or convicted for such incidents might be obtained
at follow-up. Items R-4 (alcohol) and R-5 (drugs) concern such information,
which may be available from records or discovered if the client happens to
be in jail for such an incident when located for follow-up. Inspection of
police arrest and conviction records is not recommended, because of both
privacy problems and the added resources that would be required to make such
inspections. The use of arrest rather than conviction data when final disposi-
tion of a criminal case has not yet been made is a controversial matter.

Family Strength

This is one of the more abstract and value-laden of the dimensions. There
seems to be little consensus about the meanings of "family strength" and
"family stability" or the methodology for measuring these concepts. The
approach taken by the Family Service Association of America (FSAA), which
asks for client perceptions on certain problems that could conceivably occur
in a family, appears appropriate.[1] It has been adapted for use in assessing
this dimension. The questions suggested are shown in Table 6.

Other approaches, such as that identified by Geismar,[2] utilize professional
caseworker ratings to assess the extent to which the individual and collective
needs of family members are being met. Rater subjectivity becomes a problem
in such methods. They would also require special caseworker visits to clients
who at the time of follow-up were no longer receiving services. The use of FSAA
type questions assumes that clients' perceptions of the extent and nature of
family problems are a valid, major concern. The clients' perceptions are what
is measured. The approach suggested here does not call for "objective" veri-
fication that the client had the problem(s) identified.

Child Problem Behavior

Child problem behavior may be related both to emotional and developmental difficulties and to neglect, abuse, and other external factors. Social
services are provided to families and children in part to reduce such problems.
Some authorities view problem behavior as merely the counterpart of deeper-
seated psychological or physical difficulties; they regard behavior problems
as symptoms rather than as the actual problems besetting the child. Other

---

1. Dorothy Fahs Beck and Mary Ann Jones, How to Conduct a Client Follow-Up
Study (New York: Family Service Association of America, 1974), and Beck and Jones,
Progress on Family Problems: A Nationwide Study of Clients' and Counselors' Views
on Family Agency Services (New York: Family Service Association of America, 1973).
Further discussions of the findings are presented in articles in Social Casework:
Beck and Jones, "A New Look at Clientele and Services of Family Agencies" (December
1974); Beck, "Research Findings on the Outcomes of Marital Counseling" (March
1975); and Patrick V. Riley, "Practice Changes Based on Research Findings" (April
1975). See Volume II for details.

2. Ludwig L. Geismar, Family and Community Functioning: A Manual of
Measurement for Social Work Practice and Policy (Metuchen, N.J.: The Scarecrow
Press, 1971).

TABLE 6: FAMILY STRENGTH
(PRIMARILY RELATED TO GOAL 3)

INDICATOR	QUESTION	COMMENT
17. Extent of family problems	In the past month, have you had problems with[a] 54. --your husband/wife? 55. --your children? 56. --other family members? 57. --raising children (taking care of their needs, training, discipline, and so forth)? 58. --taking care of the house, meals, or family health matters? 59. --managing money, budgeting, or credit? What is the nature of the problem? 60. --family difficulties in talking over problems, listening to each other, and sharing feelings? 61. --handling arguments and working out differences? 62. --feeling close to each other? 63. --other family problems? Would you say --almost never --sometimes --often --almost always (FOR FOLLOW-UP ONLY) 64. What was your marital status at intake? a. What is your current marital status? b. Would you say you are more satisfied or less satisfied with your marital status now than you were at intake?	The word "problems" can mean different things to different respondents; however, any effort to pinpoint the nature of the problems would necessitate many more questions. Questions 57-62 attempt to identify some types of problems, even though this may mean some degree of overlap. One way to diminish the ambiguity of responses to questions about "problems" with spouse, children, and other family members, and reduce the possibility of overlap with questions in other dimensions, is to ask about the specific nature of the problem. Another possibility is to have the interviewer tell the respondent that these questions deal only with those problems between family members that have to do with the interrelationships among them (this would exclude items like problem drinking or ill health, unless they directly affect family relationships). Further testing is necessary in order to help decide the best approach here. The questions are adapted from the Family Service Association of America questions to indicate status. The original FSAA questions indicate "change" from before services. They have been modified to indicate client's perceptions of problems in the last month. Question 59 is intended to examine the management of money and not the sufficiency of economic resources. Therefore, question 59a (see Appendix A) asks what the nature of the problem is in order to identify responses where "lack of money" is the problem so the latter can be weeded out. Although "family strength" is often interpreted as "keeping the family together," in many cases it is not clear whether staying together is preferable to separation or divorce. The client's own rating of happiness seems to be a pertinent criterion for determining whether a change in status was "better" or "worse." Therefore, question 64 should be administered at follow-up to gauge this.
18. Client's perception of degree of improvement since receiving services	When you first came to (name of agency) did you have problems with[a] 65. --your husband/wife? 66. --your children? 67. --other family members? 68. --raising children (taking care of their needs, training, discipline, etc.)? (continued)	These questions are adapted from the Family Service Association of America family counseling follow-up questionnaire. Questions 54-63 ask about the current status of various problems, whereas 65-74 are intended to obtain the client's own perception of change. These questions would be crucial if a state decides that it will administer the questionnaire only at follow-up. Lacking the before-service (continued)

a. The intensity/importance of the problem should also be sought. For each problem where the response is "sometimes" or more frequent, it may be helpful to ask the respondent "Do you consider this a major, moderate, or minor problem?"

TABLE 6, CONTINUED

INDICATOR	QUESTION	COMMENT
Client's perception of degree of improvement since receiving services (continued)	69. --taking care of the house, meals, or family health matters? 70. --managing money or with budgeting or credit? What was the nature of the problems? Are these problems now --much better --somewhat better --about the same --somewhat worse --much worse Since you started getting help from (name of agency), has there been any change in the way the members of your family 71. --talk over problems, listen to each other, share feelings? 72. --handle arguments and work out differences? 73. --feel toward each other (how close and comfortable, how you enjoy each other)? Would you say it is now --much better --somewhat better --about the same --somewhat worse --much worse 74. When you first came to (name of agency), did you have other major family problems that we have not mentioned? What was the nature of the problems? Are these problems now much better, somewhat better, about the same, somewhat worse, much worse?	"status picture," the state agency will have to depend on client assessments of the extent and direction of "change" that occurred. Clients' perceptions of improvement (here as in other dimensions) seem an important part of social service outcome assessment. Questions 54-63 can be used to identify whether the changes indicated by questions 65-74 apply to small problems or large (in terms of "absolute" levels); for example, the client may indicate considerable improvement (questions 65-74), even though the original problem may have been one that occurred only "occasionally" or "almost never" (questions 54-63). Questions 54-63 administered at intake and again at follow-up will provide estimates of "change." These can be checked for consistency by comparing them to responses obtained (at follow-up) from questions 65-74.

approaches to understanding child problems focus on behavior. Outcome measures can probably best focus on actual behavior rather than on less obvious psychological difficulties, which are more difficult to measure.

The instruments currently available for assessing child behavior are lengthy and are generally linked to specific age groups and certain categories of problems.[1] For statewide monitoring purposes it seems impractical to use different instruments for different categories of children, and so a few basic, readily observable types of "behavior problems" have been selected. The suggested questions, adapted from several sources, are shown in Table 7.

This dimension should be administered to an adult who is familiar with the child, such as the child's natural, adoptive, or foster parents. It probably should be administered in cases where the child is the primary client as well as cases where one or both parents are primary recipients of child-related services (including protective services and day care). It is not clear whether it should be administered in cases in which the principal problem is marital discord but child behavior is not directly an issue; children may or may not be affected and may or may not display problem behavior as a result of marital discord.

It is desirable, however, to obtain the perspective of children as to whether or not their situation is "satisfactory." The questions presented later on "client satisfaction" might be adapted in order to make them applicable for administration to children.

Child Welfare

Child welfare issues are complex. The "child problem behavior" dimension, already described, dealt with one such issue. In addition, the matters of child neglect, abuse, and living arrangement (placement) must be considered. Table 8 indicates the kind of information that seems needed. All of this information would be obtained from government records.

---

1. For example, the Devereux Adolescent Behavior Rating Scale seems useful for "very disturbed adolescents" rather than for normal children. The Devereux Child Behavior Rating Scale is useful for "emotionally disturbed and mentally retarded children, ages 8-12." The Devereux Elementary School Behavior Rating Scale deals with problem behavior in kindergarten through the sixth grade. (Oscar Krisen Buros, ed., The Seventh Mental Measurements Yearbook, vol. 1 (Highland Park, N.J.: Gryphon Press, 1972), pp. 67-68.) The Washington Symptom Checklist is a 76-item inventory of child behavior gleaned from complaints of parents seeking help in a child psychiatry clinic. (Herbert C. Wimberger and Robert J. Gregory, "A Behavior Checklist for Use in Child Psychiatry Clinics," Journal of the American Academy of Child Psychiatry 7 (1968):677-88.) The Child Behavior Characteristics Schedule is a 104-item checklist of "bad" and "good" behaviors. (Wisconsin, Department of Health and Social Services, Predictors of Success in Foster Care, by Patricia W. Cautley and Martha J. Aldridge (August 1973), pp. 255-56.) The National Institute of Mental Health's Handbook of Psychiatric Rating Scales, 2nd ed. (1973), identifies other scales for rating child behavior and symptoms.

TABLE 7: CHILD PROBLEM BEHAVIOR
(PRIMARILY RELATED TO GOAL 3)

INDICATOR	QUESTION	COMMENT
19. Extent of child problem behavior	75. How many children do you have who are below the age of eighteen? What are their names and ages? In the past month, how often did (name of child) 76. --show anger by having tantrums? 77. --fight or hurt peers while playing with them? 78. --act withdrawn and uncommunicative? 79. --steal things from others? 80. --resist or refuse to do what was asked? 81. --destroy property, commit vandalism? 82. --play hooky? --almost never --sometimes --often --almost always 83. In the past month, did (name of child) ever run away from home? How many times? 84. Was (name of child) arrested in the past twelve months? 85. Is (name of child) currently in school? a. In the past twelve months, has (name of child) failed a course, failed a grade, been suspended or expelled, or none of these? b. In the past month, have you had complaints from (name of child)'s teacher about behavior in class--almost never, sometimes, often, almost always?	Where there is more than one child this dimension should be administered for each child. (See Chapter 2 for details of which dimensions should be administered to each client group.) These questions are to be administered by an interviewer to the parent (or, in some cases, the foster parent or teacher). Some of the questions may not be applicable for very young children. The response categories (almost never, sometimes, . . .) are somewhat vague and need to be further defined in future versions. In addition, it might also be desirable to ask respondents, for each problem, whether they feel the problem to be major or minor; frequency of incidents may not always be an adequate proxy for severity.
20. Respondent's perception of degree of improvement since receiving services.	Since you started getting help from (name of agency), has there been a change in (name of child) with respect to 86. --showing anger by having tantrums? 87. --fighting or hurting peers when playing with them? 88. --acting withdrawn and uncommunicative? 89. --stealing things from others? 90. --resisting or refusing to do what is asked? 91. --destroying property, committing vandalism? 92. --playing hooky? Would you say the child is now --much better --somewhat better --about the same --somewhat worse --much worse	Questions 86-92 would be essential if the government decides only to do a follow-up survey and not also obtain information at intake (as needed for questions 76-85 to indicate change). The information obtained at intake from questions 76-82 on the frequency of the incidents can be used to indicate whether the responses obtained from questions 86-92 pertain to small or large problems. The two sets of questions (76-85 and 86-92) also serve as a consistency check on one another.

TABLE 8: CHILD WELFARE
(PRIMARILY RELATED TO GOAL 3)

INDICATOR	QUESTION	COMMENT
21. Child abuse recidivism	R-6. Frequency and severity of recurrence of abuse or neglect --No indication of child abuse or neglect --Reported but unconfirmed case of child abuse or neglect --Confirmed case of child abuse or neglect --Child removed from home temporarily due to recurrence of abuse or neglect --Child removed from home permanently due to recurrence of abuse or neglect --Injury to child resulting from abuse --Death of child as a result of abuse	This information is to be gathered for those cases in the sample that have a recorded known child abuse history whether the name drawn in the sample is that of the child or that of the parent. These indicators could also be adapted to cases of abused or neglected adults. Note that this indicator covers only recidivism, not the frequency of child abuse cases. Thus, the concern addressed here is with repeat situations. To the extent that social service agencies have a responsibility for preventing new (not repeat) cases, reported child abuse cases would be the best currently available indicator.
22. Timeliness of placement	R-7. Timeliness of placement --Child placed in adoptive home within ninety days after decision to seek adoptive placement --For "hard to place" child: child placed in adoptive home within one year after decision to seek adoptive placement --Child's adoption legally completed within one year	Another issue in the case of the placement of a child (or adult) is the waiting time involved once the decision about placement has been made. Some examples of such indicators are given in R-7; these have been adapted from the effectiveness measures used by the Milwaukee County Department of Public Welfare. In each of these cases, a "percentage" is calculated--for example, percent of children placed in an adoptive home within ninety days after decision to seek adoptive placement, divided by number of children for whom adoptive placement is planned.
23. Improvement in child's living situation	R-8. Placement status Improvement: --Institution to own home --Foster home to own home --Institution to adoption --Foster home to adoption --Institution to foster home No Change: --Continuing in own home --Continuing in foster home --Continuing in institution --Continuing in adoption Deterioration: --Changed foster home; foster parents unable to continue care --Changed foster home; incompatible foster home --Went from foster home to institution --Child transferred to another institution for reasons other than age or improvement in conditions --Child placed in institution within twelve months of being discharged from another institution (recidivism)	These data seek to identify changes in the placement status of a child--whether there was a change, and if so, whether it appeared to be an improvement or a deterioration. The assumption here is that there is an ascending hierarchy of placements in order of preference--from an institution, foster home, adoption, to the child's own home. It is likely that this order is not always the most suitable for a particular client; for example, a child may be better off somewhere other than the child's own home. The hierarchy assumes that the child's home is preferable only if the unsuitable conditions that warranted social service efforts have been greatly ameliorated.

In addition to information on abuse and placement and that obtained on child behavior problems, other information seems desirable to obtain a full perspective. This includes data on the child's physical health and mental distress and the child's satisfaction with placement. Thus, the sections of the questionnaire dealing with the physical health, mental distress, and client satisfaction of adults should be adapted in order to assess the same dimensions for children (at least for those old enough to respond for themselves). These adaptations may not be difficult to prepare. The satisfaction of foster or adoptive parents is another element that should perhaps also be considered in assessing adequacy of placement.

Client Satisfaction

While some may contend that clients' own perceptions of personal improvement or of conditions around them may be erroneous, clients' perceptions (whether "right" or "wrong") are likely to be of considerable importance to most social service agencies and their governments.[1] There are several aspects of "client satisfaction" that can appropriately be assessed:

1. The client's perceptions of change--

    a. In terms of "overall" change (question 94);
    b. In terms of changes in specific problems of the client (for example, ability to communicate with members of one's family, which may be improved by family counseling services) (questions 23, 41, 64-74, and 86-92);
    c. In terms of the extent to which the client believes that any change that did occur was due to the help provided by the social service agency (question 95).

2. Specific aspects of service quality, such as whether the client has been treated with dignity and courtesy, whether the agency was accessible, and so on (questions 96-103).

3. Whether the amenities of care provided in institutions were satisfactory (questions 105-122--discussed in next section).

The information and associated questions identified in this section pertains to items 1a, 1c, and 2. Client satisfaction questions on specific problems are contained in the particular dimension that includes the problems.[2] Satisfaction questions on amenities of care in institutions will be presented in the next section of this chapter.

---

1. Milwaukee, Wisconsin, has an ordinance that requires its Department of Public Welfare to give all clients or their relatives the opportunity once a year to rate the services provided.

2. Such questions are particularly useful when a more "objective" approach to assessing client change appears inadequate--for example, in assessing family strength or child problem behavior, rather than economic self-support or physical health.

TABLE 9: CLIENT SATISFACTION

INDICATOR	QUESTION	COMMENT
24. Client's perception of degree of overall improvement since receiving services	93. What are the problems that led you to get help from (name of agency) since (date)? 94. Considering the problems that led you to get help from (name of agency), how would you say things are now? --much better --somewhat better --about the same --somewhat worse --better in some ways but worse in others (please explain)	Asking the client to explain if things have become "worse" provides interpretive information. For questions 94, 95, and 96, the state may, in addition, want an explanation even if things have stayed the same or become better.
25. Client's perception of the degree to which services have helped	95. Do you feel the help you received from (name of agency) influenced the changes you mentioned above? --helped a great deal --helped some --made no difference --made things worse (please explain)	
26. Client's satisfaction with various aspects of services provided	96. In general, how do you feel about the services provided by (name of agency) since (date)? --very satisfied --satisfied --no particular feelings one way or the other --not satisfied (please explain) Did you have any problems with 97. --fees? 98. --waiting time for filling out forms, getting help, etc.? 99. --location of services? 100. --appointment times with your caseworker? 101. --changes in caseworkers? 102. --paperwork? 103. --the way caseworkers treated you? Was there --no problem --a small problem (please explain) --a major problem (please explain) 104. Are there any other comments you would like to make about the quality of the services you received?	

The questions shown in Table 9 are appropriate for use only at follow-up, not at entry, since they ask about conditions occurring after services have been provided.

The questions in Table 9 ask about overall problems as well as such specific matters as: fees, waiting times, accessibility of services, treatment by caseworkers, and amount of paperwork. Questions could also be asked about a number of other specific matters, such as client participation in the planning of objectives and services, the quality of clients' communication with caseworkers, and client initiative in making and carrying out service plans. These latter elements appear to be "intermediate" outputs rather than outcomes and hence have not been included. However, some agencies may want to include such questions and correlate the resulting information with the outcome data.

The questions in this table have been adapted from the work of the Family Service Association of America.[1]

Amenities of Care in Institutions

For clients who are institutionalized for prolonged periods of time, degree of satisfaction with the various amenties of care appears to be an important matter. Even though institutional care may not generally be funded by Title XX, social service agencies are concerned about conditions in institutions, and the importance of these conditions seems implied by the "appropriateness of care" wording of Title XX's Goal 5.

The questions in Table 10 have been developed by us from observations as to the aspects of care likely to be important to institutionalized clients. These questions were not included in the client satisfaction questionnaire pretested by the state of North Carolina.

The questions would be administered by trained interviewers to clients able to answer questions; in other cases, they could be asked of friends or close relatives familiar with the clients' situations. To encourage candid responses, some form of a "secret ballot" approach could be used so that responses would not be identified with individual clients.

---

1. See, for example, Beck and Jones, How to Conduct a Client Follow-Up Study and Progress on Family Problems.

2. Each government will have to decide on a definition of "institution." Various criteria for defining an institution have been suggested: (1) number of residents; (2) overnight stay by clients; (3) whether a client can be mandated by the state to live there, etc. The state of North Carolina defines an institution for the purposes of Title XX services as "a facility that is established to serve a particular purpose and is required by state law to be provided and maintained by the state, or is defined in the Federal Register No. 228.44 as an institution."

TABLE 10: AMENITIES OF CARE IN INSTITUTIONS
(PRIMARILY FOR GOAL 5)

INDICATOR	QUESTION	COMMENT
27. Client's satisfaction with services provided in the institution	In the past two weeks 105. --have your meals been served hot enough? 106. --did you like the taste of the food served here? 107. --did you get enough food to eat? 108. --did you get clean sheets and towels often enough? 109. --were your clothes washed often enough? 110. --did you have sufficient opportunities to socialize with the other people here? 111. --have you had enough opportunities for recreation? 112. --when you wanted something done, did the staff members respond to your needs? 113. --did the staff members treat you politely and with respect? 114. --did you get medical care when you needed it? 116. In the past year, have you made an official complaint about anything here? a. Was anything done about it? Please describe what happened. b. Do you know anyone who made an official complaint about something here during the past year? c. Was anything done about it? Please describe what happened. In the past two weeks 117. --have you liked the way (name of institution) looked (appearance, cleanness, general maintenance)? 118. --was the temperature of your room comfortable? 119. --has there been anything you especially liked about this place? 120. --has there been anything you especailly disliked about this place? 121. In general, to what extent are you satisfied with (name of institution)? --very satisfied --satisfied --dissatisfied --very dissatisfied 122. (FOR THOSE WHO MOVED TO THE CURRENT INSTITUTION DURING THE PREVIOUS YEAR) How would you compare (name of institution) to where you were before? --current place is far better --current place is somewhat better --current place is better in some ways and worse in others --current place is worse	Some questions could be added about the clients' perception of privacy and autonomy and whether clients feel that their personal possessions are safe. Question 122 is most appropriate for clients who have transferred to the institution during the past year. It may also be appropriate for clients who have moved from one place of residence to another during the past year (for example, aged persons who have moved to group homes), even if the state may not consider these homes as institutions.

Chapter 2

SOME ISSUES IN USING THE CLIENT-OUTCOME QUESTIONNAIRE

In this chapter three important issues involving the questionnaire and its use are discussed: (1) which sections of the client-outcome questionnaire are appropriate to administer to which types of clients; (2) what types of procedures are likely to be appropriate for scoring the data obtained so as to provide summary information on client conditions; and (3) how can the questionnaire data be used to help provide information on "appropriateness of care" for assessing Title XX Goals 4 and 5.

Which Sections of the Questionnaire Are Appropriate to be Administered to Which Types of Clients?

The questionnaire consists of several "modules," each dealing with one dimension--economic self-support, physical health, mental distress, etc. Not all "modules" should be administered to each client. This section provides some preliminary suggestions as to which modules are appropriate for which client groups.

There is considerable diversity in client problems and situations. Hence it is impossible to give interviewers simple instructions on the administration of the questionnaire that will cover every eventuality. Interviewers should be well trained and be permitted to use judgment in situations that are not covered by the instructions.

Four major client groups should be considered when making judgments about administering the various sections of the questionnaire. These four groups are:

1. Institutionalized Adults.
2. Other Adults. (This includes those with self-support problems, aged persons, neglected and abused adults, the handicapped, the retarded, and disturbed persons--who are living in the community.)
3. Institutionalized Children.
4. Other Children. (This includes neglected or abused children, including those who are being placed or are being considered for placement.)

There are a number of difficult issues here, especially in cases involving children. For example, should a child be interviewed to obtain information on the child's perceptions of health, alcohol and drug abuse, and satisfaction? If so, at what age? Should a parent or guardian be asked in some cases to respond for the child on matters such as the child's health, or use of alcohol and drugs? Should parents or guardians be asked about their own status with regard to health, family strength, satisfaction, and the like on the assumption that the parent/guardian is either a secondary client or that these elements are part of a "good" placement for the child?

The following are preliminary thoughts on the choice of sections of the questionnaire to be administered to each group. The underlying philosophy here is that the information obtained should not necessarily be limited to information directly applicable to the client's primary goal but should cover all problem areas (within the scope of social service agency interests) that are of concern to the client.

Institutionalized Adults. The following sections seem appropriate:

- Portions of Economic Self-Support
  The questions on current employment status and extent of earnings are not applicable, but the extent of other sources of income is relevant.
- Ability to Undertake Activities of Daily Living (Personal and Instrumental)
- Physical Health
- Mental Distress
- Client Satisfaction
- Amenities of Care in Institutions

The section on alcohol and drug abuse does not appear relevant, even though the client may have been an alcoholic or drug abuser before entering the institution, since there would probably be little access to these substances in institutions.

Other Adults. The following sections seem appropriate:

- Economic Self-Support
  If the adult is retired, or too aged or handicapped to work, the employment status or earnings questions will be inappropriate; however, the other self-support questions are relevant because the extent of dependency upon public assistance is an issue. In cases in which the problems relate to self-support, the entire dimension will be appropriate.
- Ability to Undertake Activities of Daily Living
  For healthy adults, these questions are not likely to be needed. The difficulty is that such problems may not always be obvious. The interviewer probably should be allowed some flexibility if the situation is such that administration of some, or all, of these questions is clearly inappropriate. However, if there is any doubt, the questions should be administered; the questions take little time for healthy adults.

Some aged persons are going to deteriorate regardless of services provided and, at best, services may only decrease the rate
of deterioration. The questions are useful for assessing both
improvement and degree to which deterioration occurs.

- Physical Health
- Mental Distress
- Alcohol and Drug Abuse
- Family Strength
  This should be administered to adults who live with family
  members. The assumption here is that family strength questions
  are appropriate in cases where there is a possibility that a
  high amount of family discord in the home detracts from the
  client's well-being.
- Client Satisfaction

In addition to the above, the questions on child problem behavior probably
should be administered to adults who receive child-related services, including
child-abuse-related services. In such cases, information should also be
collected regarding child welfare. These sections possibly should also be
administered to clients who receive marriage counseling and have children,
since marital discord can affect child behavior. If there is more than one
child in the family, the parent(s) should be asked about the problem behavior
of each child. In some cases the client will already have been identified
as having problems with a certain child or children. In other cases, such as
day-care-only clients, there might be no such indication.

Institutionalized Children. If it is believed (as seems to be generally
implicit in current measurement practices) that the very fact that the child
is in an institution at the time of follow-up makes the placement a failure,
by definition, it would not be necessary to obtain any further information,
such as the progress of the child in the institution.

If, however, the government also wishes to assess the child's well-being
on such dimensions as health and problem behavior, it is appropriate to administer some of the sections of the questionnaire. The economic self-support and
family strength questions do not seem appropriate for outcome assessment.
(The family strength questions would be appropriate for the family from which
the child was removed.) The focus, here, however, is on the child and the child's
own condition and current living environment. The following sections seem
appropriate:

- Ability to Undertake Personal Activities of Daily Living
  This would be administered to either the child or the "house-
  parent" or nearest equivalent, depending on the child's age
  and condition; in either case, the questions need partial
  modification. The house-parent would be asked about the child's
  condition, not the parent's.
- Physical Health
  If old enough to respond, the child could be administered a
  modified version; otherwise, the "house-parent" would be asked
  to respond for the child.

- Mental Distress
  If old enough to respond, the child could be adminstered a modified version.
- Alcohol and Drug Abuse
  This would be administered only to older children (perhaps twelve-year-olds and above).
- Child Problem Behavior
  This would be administered to the "house-parent" or nearest equivalent.
- Child Welfare
  This would be obtained from case records.
- Amenities of Care in Institutions
  If old enough to respond, the child should be administered a modified version.

Other Children. These are cases in which the child's name is drawn as the "primary client" and the child is living in a noninstitutionalized setting with parents, guardians or foster parents.

If it is believed that the major issue is the type of placement (whether in a foster home, adoptive residence, or with natural parents) and that knowing in which type the child has been placed is sufficient to determine the quality of the placement, it would be unnecessary to administer any other part of the questionnaire to these clients. The information obtained from records for the Child Welfare dimension, items R-6, 7, and 8 in Appendix A, would be sufficient. If the government also wishes to consider the child's well-being on such issues as health and problem behavior, however, it is appropriate to administer various other sections of the questionnaire.[1] Some information would be obtained from the parent or guardian; if the child is old enough to respond, other information would be obtained from the child. The following sections seem appropriate:

- Economic Self-Support
  This section would be administered to the parent or guardian, on the assumption that the economic well-being of a family is an important part of a "good" situation for a child. Only those questions pertaining to the current income of the family seem relevant.
- Ability to Undertake Personal Activities of Daily Living
  Only the "personal" and not the "instrumental" activites of daily living questions would be administered, since children, by definition, are not expected to be able to perform the instrumental activities of daily living. Normal children are often slower in some areas than others, and only where it is known that the child has "developmental" problems does

---

1. A question raised in North Carolina was whether an interviewer should report a hitherto unknown situation of abuse or neglect discovered during an interview. The same problem could arise in other dimensions, such as the alcohol and drug abuse questions. In general, interviewer confidentiality obligations are similar to those of doctors and lawyers. However, this issue needs further consideration.

it seem to make sense to use the questions on personal activities. The questions should be asked of either the child or the parent/guardian, depending on the child's age and condition. In either case, the questions would need partial modification. The parents/guardians would be asked about the children's conditions, not their own.

- Physical Health
  If old enough to respond, the child could be given a modified version; otherwise, the parent/guardian would be asked to respond for the child.

- Mental Distress
  If old enough to respond, the child could be given a modified version.[1]

- Alcohol and Drug Abuse
  This would be administered only to older children (perhaps twelve years old and above).

- Family Strength
  This might be administered to the parent/guardian on the assumption that these conditions can significantly affect the appropriateness of the placement. However, it could be awkward to administer it to persons who were not or had not been clients. The questions would need to be modified for this use.

- Child Problem Behavior
  This would be administered to the parent/guardian.

- Child Welfare
  This would be obtained from case records.

- Client Satisfaction
  If old enough to respond, this section should be administered to the child. It would be modified somewhat for this purpose. For children placed in other than their homes, it also seems appropriate to administer this dimension to the parent/guardian.[2]

What Procedures Are Appropriate for Scoring the Findings to Provide Summary Results?

The illustrative questionnaire shown in Appendix A contains well over one hundred items of information. Staff analysts are likely to be interested in examining responses on a question-by-question basis. However, for middle- and upper-level management purposes, such a quantity of information would clearly be excessively cumbersome. The information should be summarized

---

1. If one subscribes to the view that the physical (and mental) health of the parents are crucial elements in a "good" situation for the child, it would make sense also to administer a version of this dimension to the parent asking about the health of the parent.

2. Many of the members of North Carolina's advisory committee felt it desirable to interview small children, even as young as five years old, on the satisfaction questions--especially in adoption and foster care services. The issue of whether guardians would let children be interviewed then arises. Of concern, also, is the possibility that children may be highly affected by recent events. In general, if the sample is large enough such events seem likely to cancel one another.

to provide an overall perspective on client outcomes. Thus, procedures are needed to aggregate the responses to individual questions so that overall scores can be obtained.

As indicated in Exhibit 1, it is suggested that information on the individual questions be combined into scores for the thirty indicators and that indicator scores be combined into scores for each dimension. Dimension scores could also be combined to provide overall scores for each goal, or even into one overall score per client. The problem is how to tally the information in a meaningful, reliable manner so that the resulting scores represent significant differences in client conditions, whether for individual indicators, dimensions, goals, or overall scores.

No specific scoring procedures have yet been developed for the questions in Appendix A. Considerable effort is needed to develop scoring procedures on this or any questionnaire that contains a large number of items. Such scoring can be developed in various technically sophisticated ways. Some version of the following approach seems appropriate to develop the scoring procedure.

A group of "experts" (preferably a variety of professionals in the field of social services, including agency representatives, caseworkers, and perhaps client representatives) would assess the data provided on a test set of questionnaires. For each completed questionnaire the experts would provide ratings on each indicator, dimension, goal, or overall rating that was being sought, based on their own interpretation of the questionnaires and using whatever method they wished. These ratings by the experts would be used in the following two ways: (a) the ratings of the experts would be correlated with the individual responses on the questionnaire to derive weights for individual questions; (b) for each preselected scoring procedure candidate, the procedure's summary ratings would be compared against the experts' ratings to determine whether any of the candidate procedures reasonably reproduced the experts' ratings.

It is assumed in the above procedures that a government would find it impractical to use a set of experts to rate large numbers of clients annually and that some relatively mechanical scoring procedure would be necessary. In any case, it is desirable to have a reasonably standardized set of scoring rules so that scores are not unduly sensitive to the person doing the scoring.

There are at least three specific types of candidate procedures that appear appropriate for such scoring. Any one, or some combination of the three, could be used:

1. Assign weights to each response category for each question and then assign weights to each question in order to derive an indicator score. For example, the ten mental distress questions (questions 24-33 of Appendix A) might be scored by assigning values of 0 to 3, respectively, to the four response categories (for instance, "never had the problem" would be scored "0," "once or twice" would be scored "1," and so on). Then, assuming equal weights for each question, the scores on each question would be added to provide a total

score for the ten questions, thus giving a score for the indicator "index of mental distress" (see Exhibit 1).[1]

To aggregate the scores into a small number of categories of client conditions, a set of four categories might be defined, perhaps by the panel of experts noted above, as, for example:

No problem	0-7
Small problem	8-14
Moderate problem	15-21
Major problem	22-30

The actual score tallied would then determine into which category the client would fall. Similarly, weights could be assigned to each indicator in order to aggregate more than one indicator into a dimension score, and so on.

2. Provide a set of rules for grouping the clients into various pre-established categories of outcomes. For example, for an aggregate child problem behavior rating, rules might be designed to combine the responses on individual questions for each client into one of the four categories noted above using rules such as the following:

"No problem": A child almost never commits any problem behavior and never has run away from home.

"Small problem": A child often has tantrums, almost never steals, withdraws, plays truant, sometimes disobeys, destroys property, fights, and never has run away.

3. Obtain a community "norm" against which the clients' responses can be compared. This is appropriate for some but not all of the indicators. For example, if the mental distress questions are administered to a sample of citizens throughout the state, the average score could be used as a norm against which client conditions at follow-up could be compared.[2]

When clients' conditions at follow-up are being compared with their conditions at entry, another scoring option is to identify the number of items in which the client has improved and the number of items in which the client has deteriorated. The net total of plus and minus scores would be considered as the change score.[3]

---

1. This is part of the scoring procedure used by the Denver Community Mental Health team for the mental distress portion of its questionnaire.

2. This procedure was used by the Denver Community Mental Health team using a norm based on scores from a sample of the Denver population.

3. This procedure has been used by the Family Service Association of America to score its client follow-up questionnaire. As in the FSAA work, this procedure could be used on the questions that ask clients for their perceptions as to whether their situation has improved since they received services (such as the family strength questions), as well as for items where pre and postcondition scores are obtained.

"Change scores" reflecting changes in clients before and after receiving services seem useful and practical, but there are some additional methodological issues. It can be argued that persons with before-treatment scores below the average will, regardless of treatment, tend to improve relative to those who initially scored above the average--the phenomenon of "regression toward the mean."[1] This argument is applied most often when clients are assessed on changes in written test scores. The extent to which this argument applies to social service clients is not clear. As discussed elsewhere in this report, grouping clients by their apparent condition at entry (by "client difficulty") using the clients' entry scores is recommended. If this is done, outcomes can be provided separately for each difficulty-group, and this "regression-effect" problem should then not be so important a concern.

Fortunately, scoring the findings from the sampling of clients does not require great precision. As discussed in Chapter 4, however, the scoring procedures will have to be thoroughly tested to certify their ability to discriminate reasonably among clients with different levels of outcomes.

Appropriateness of Care [2]

Goals 4 and 5 of Title XX are concerned with the appropriateness of care provided. Both goals require the collection of similar information. Goal 4 focuses on the avoidance of unnecessary institutionalization of clients, while Goal 5 is concerned primarily with clients who are not institutionalized and nonclients in the community who need to be institutionalized. (This goal can also be interpreted to include adequate service for clients who are appropriately institutionalized; the "amenities of care" dimension in Chapter 1 is included to consider this purpose.)

The determination of whether a client is receiving "appropriate" care is a complex one, and one that different people may disagree on from case to case. The procedures discussed here, although not validated, can be used to help make such decisions, but we know of no procedure as yet developed that can make such determinations in a systematic, objective, reliable manner. Considerable work is likely to be needed before such a procedure is developed.

For both Goals 4 and 5, "appropriateness of care" assessment appears to require only information pertaining to a client's status at follow-up. It does not appear necessary to compare a client's condition at follow-up with condition at entry.

Goal 4

The objective of the procedures discussed below is to obtain estimates of--

---

1. Jim Nunnally, "The Study of Change in Evaluation Research," in Handbook of Evaluation Research, ed. Marcia Guttentag and Elmer L. Struening (Beverly Hills: Sage Publications, 1975), vol. 1, p. 112.

2. The discussion is limited to adult clients.

1. The percentage of institutionalized adult clients who could be deinstitutionalized if services could be expanded in some way to assist them in the community,[1] and

2. The percentage of institutionalized adult clients who are clearly inappropriately institutionalized.

The following steps are suggested:

1. Assess institutionalized clients (or at least a sample of them) in terms of the findings on those dimensions of the client outcome-monitoring instrument relevant to determining self-sufficiency, as supplemented by professional judgments. The assessment would cover clients' ability to undertake both the personal and instrumental activities of daily living. In cases involving clients unable to answer, the questions would be administered to another person, such as a relative, a friend, or even a staff member, if necessary. Alternatively, it might be appropriate and efficient to have staff members rather than clients themselves provide the ratings.

The assessment would also cover the physical health of clients. Are the clients medically ill, to the point at which daily skilled nursing or essential services available only in an institution are necessary in order to maintain their health? Would the clients be unable to deal with their own health needs, and would no one (relative, friend, visiting nurse) be available to care for them in their homes? Most of these questions do not seem appropriate for administration to institutionalized adult clients; hence ratings by medical personnel at the institutions would be necessary.

The mental state of clients also should be assessed:

--Are the clients psychotic?
--Are they likely to set fire to the residence?
--Are the clients likely to disturb others, to the extent that police intervention becomes necessary?
--Would the clients frighten others living in the same home by strange behavior or violent outbursts of temper?
--Have the clients shown serious suicidal tendencies?

In addition, there are such issues as whether clients, if living alone, would forget to eat, neglect self-care to the point of endangering their health, or be highly disoriented as to time and place, and whether clients, if living with other persons, would request and accept help.

These are some of the questions that have to be considered in an assessment of the ability of institutionalized clients to live in the community. The mental distress questions, administered to those clients able to respond, would probably aid in this assessment, but an assessment by a professional also seems needed. Such assessments are probably made routinely for most clients in order to certify the appropriateness of institutionalization; however, it is not clear whether the criteria used from agency to agency and

---

1. This indicator is one that is less likely to be directly correctable by the social service agency without more funds or resources.

community to community are consistent. It would be useful to systematize standards and thereby improve the quality of decisions about institutionalization.

  2. Depending on deficiencies noted in the above assessments, information would then be needed on:

>   --Whether each client has private assistance that could be relied on in a private setting when needed by the client.
>   --If not, whether a client's needs could be met by public services (homemaker services and the like).

Note that, given sufficient private (or public) resources, no individual needs to be institutionalized except in extreme cases. For example, a sufficiently wealthy family may choose to pay for round-the-clock professional care for dependent persons, including extremely dependent ones, in order to keep them at home. This situation does not often apply, however, to social service clients.

  More specific information will be needed on the resources available to the client. Such information, obtained from the client and/or relatives, would include:

>   --Information on the availability of a person(s) to assist the client in the performance of those activities of daily living with which he/she needs help.
>   --The frequency with which such help is available.
>   --The dependability of such help.

Information should also be obtained as to whether the services needed for keeping the client in the community would be available from agencies (public or private) in the community.

  3. Once such information is obtained, the state still has the task of combining each of the above elements into a coherent set of criteria for determining when institutionalization is appropriate. This is probably the most difficult task since it involves making policy-based assumptions in addition to scoring difficulties.[1] A number of sample cases might be examined in order to arrive at a set of rules that is feasible and meaningful.

  In addition, there are other issues to be considered in determining appropriateness of care. For instance, consider the case of a mildly senile,

---

  1. For instance, consider the study conducted by the London Borough of Greenwich (discussed further in Volume II of this work). Each respondent was rated on a physical index, a mental index, and a social index. Based on responses for each index, rules were developed for defining the need for residential care. One of the rules was as follows: "One example of a person in need of residential care according to this definition would be someone who was bedfast or had difficulty making a hot drink, and either lived alone or would have had no help if ill." Quentin Thompson, "Assessing the Need for Residential Care for the Elderly," Quarterly Bulletin of the Intelligence Unit (Greater London Council), no. 24 (September 1973), pp. 37-42.

institutionalized client who wants to return home. The client's ratings on
activities of daily living and physical and mental health conditions might
show no reason why the person should not return home if some daily assistance
can be obtained from members of the client's family. If the latter are un-
willing or unable to provide such support, however, is institutionalization
appropriate or not? This question has to be considered in terms of the financial cost to the state, the needs and well-being of the client, and the
psychic cost to other members of the family.

The burden on families can be viewed as a relevant dimension of the outcomes of social services, but procedures for directly measuring family burden
are not included in this study. Some data collection instruments that could
be adapted for such purposes have been developed in the mental health field.[1]

Goal 5

Goal 5 deals with the issue of whether those in need of institutional
care get it. Three types of information would appear to be of concern here:

1. A determination of the extent to which there are citizens currently
not receiving social services but needing institutional care. A statewide
needs-assessment questionnaire appears to be an appropriate procedure for
obtaining at least rough estimates of the number of such citizens. This procedure and its alternatives are discussed at greater length in Chapter 5.

2. In addition, information is needed on the extent to which active
social service clients living in the community need institutional care.
Candidates for institutionalization might be found among aged, mentally
retarded, severely handicapped, and emotionally disturbed clients.

As with Goal 4, the questions to be answered revolve around the ability
of each client to perform the personal and instrumental activities of daily
living, the availability of resources, physical health, mental health, and
so on. The issues are similar to those of Goal 4, but they need to be interpreted in light of the living situation in the client's home.[2]

3. Goal 5 also seems to include the issue of whether those who are
appropriately institutionalized are receiving adequate services. Chapter 1
contains a discussion of a set of questions on "amenities of care in institutions" that could be used in assessing this aspect of the goal. These
questions would be administered to those clients able to respond.

---

1. A discussion of "family burden" and illustrations of data collection
instruments to determine it are presented in the Urban Institute's forthcoming
(1977) report Monitoring the Outcomes of State Mental Health Treatment Programs:
Some Initial Suggestions, by Alfred H. Schainblatt.

2. Occasionally there are cases involving a client who insists on living
in the community but is incapable of doing so safely. Such situations tend
to involve legal and psychiatric issues which require expert professional
judgment.

Chapter 3

OTHER PROCEDURAL ISSUES IN CLIENT OUTCOME MONITORING

The major procedural issues discussed in this chapter are:[1]

1. For how many clients should information be obtained--
    that is, how large should the sample be? Which client
    groups should be distinguished when assessing outcomes?

2. How should the clients for whom the information is to
    be obtained be identified and selected?

3. When should the information be obtained on each client?

4. Who should administer the questionnaire?

5. How should it be administered--that is, by mail, by
    telephone, or in person?

6. How can the "confidentiality and privacy" issues be
    properly handled?

In the discussion of these six issues that follows, two points serve
as general guidelines:

1. The data obtained should be reasonably representative of the major
social services clientele.

2. Costs should be minimized. This is a major constraint, for the annual
cost for the procedure is likely to be at least $50,000 to $100,000.[2] This
is not necessarily all out-of-pocket cost; much depends on the extent to which
appropriate personnel are available to help in the effort and the extent to
which existing government data systems can be utilized.

---

1. A useful discussion and a somewhat different perspective on some of
these issues is contained in the Northwest Federation for Human Services
draft, "Microdata Sampling Systems: A Proposed Measurement Design" (Boise,
Idaho, April 19, 1976).

2. This figure is based on similar efforts in other service areas, such
as mental health.

1. <u>For how many clients should information be obtained?</u> <u>Which client</u>
   <u>groups should be distinguished when assessing outcomes?</u>

In general, 100 percent coverage will not be feasible for most states
because of the large total number of social service clients. Hence, this
discussion assumes that the outcomes of only a sample of the clients will be
assessed each year.

For which client groups should the data be aggregated? There are numerous categories in which state (and local) officials are likely to be interested.
These include:

> --Geographical location of the clients
> --Primary goal for each client
> --Type of client problem
> --Type of program (service) received
> --Type of delivery (for example, contract services
>   versus direct services)
> --Various personal characteristics, such as age group,
>   sex, income, and race.

The geographical categorization could include any of the following:

> --Social service administrative regions
> --Counties (but samples large enough to yield meaningful
>   data for each county in a state would often result in
>   excessively large and expensive samples)
> --Some grouping of counties, perhaps on the basis of
>   population (or better yet, on the basis of number of
>   clients)
> --Type of region, such as rural, urban, suburban.

A minimum number of clients will have to be included in the sample for
each client group for which reasonably precise information is desired. The
key issue in determining this number is the level of precision sought by the
state. The larger the sample, the greater the likelihood that the findings [2]
from the sample will be close to the characteristics of the total clientele.
However, it is by no means clear what level of accuracy is needed.

---

1. A state or county probably will not want to include in the client outcome-
monitoring process clients whose only contact is with information and referral
personnel. The criterion for deciding who is a "client" could be the filling
out of an intake form and the administering of the mechanics for officially
"opening" the case. Inclusion of information-and-referral-only clients would
probably result in excessive numbers of clients who had been provided little in
the way of social services, at the expense of clients who had received significant amounts of assistance. It is recommended that information-and-referral-
only clients not be included in the main sample, but be given an opportunity
to fill out a short client-satisfaction questionnaire.

2. Note, however, that nonsampling errors (such as those from poor interviewing, or poor questionnaire wording) are also major problems in ensuring
the accuracy of outcome measurement findings.

In similar work the authors have often used, somewhat arbitrarily, a sample size of 100 as a basic minimum. This means that if, for example, the findings were that 20 percent of the 100 achieved a certain amount of improvement, there is roughly a 90 percent chance that for the whole of even a large universe of clients the percentage of clients achieving improvement would fall within a range of approximately 13.4 percent to 26.6 percent (+ 6.6 percentage points). This is by no means ideal, but for many purposes it is likely to be acceptable.[1] Even smaller samples can be used, but they will not permit officials to draw conclusions with any great confidence unless the observed differences between groups are quite large.

The sample size is determined in part by the number of subgroups for which outcome information is desired. If only one characteristic, such as age, will be used to group clients at any one time in the analysis, then the necessary sample size is determined by the characteristic that has the most subgroups. For example, if a state wants to subdivide a total sample for one purpose into four age groups, for another purpose into ten types of programs, and for a third purpose into fourteen geographical areas, then geographical area would be the characteristic which determines sample size. If 100 clients per subgroup were desired, then the sample would have to include 1,400 clients.

If a state, however, wants to obtain tabulations using more than one characteristic at a time, the required sample size is multiplied. For example, if a state wants to obtain information on ten types of programs in each of fourteen geographical areas, 140 different samples would be required. If each sample were to have 100 clients, the total sample required would be 14,000!

Although availability of funds and desire for precision will differ somewhat among states, it is suggested that states consider using annual total sample sizes of approximately 2,000 to 3,000 clients. This would permit a state to make rough comparisons among perhaps twenty to thirty of its geographic areas. Some of the largest counties (in terms of numbers of clients) could probably be designated as specific areas, with the remaining areas being counties grouped geographically, or according to rural or urban designations, or by some other characteristic felt to be significant.

2. How should the clients for whom the information is to be obtained be identified and selected?

The intention should be to draw samples so that each client has, to the extent possible, an equal chance of being included in the sample. In practice, there are many complications.

---

1. For samples of 500, the 90 percent confidence range would be roughly 17.0 percent to 23.0 percent (+ 3.0 percentage points); and for a sample of 1,000, 17.9 percent to 22.1 percent (+ 2.1 percentage points)--both of which should be quite adequate for most purposes. Even 80 percent confidence levels may be adequate for state officials. If so, smaller samples could be used, or the larger sample sizes could be used but with narrower confidence ranges; for example, for a sample of 100, the 80 percent confidence interval would be approximately 14.9 percent to 25.1 percent (+ 5.1 percentage points rather than + 6.6).

First, there is the matter of identifying the list(s) from which samples are to be drawn. If the state has a computerized reporting system in operation, and if reporting from the county offices is adequate, a reliable list of clients from which to draw the sample should be available. Where such a reporting system is not yet in existence (as will probably often be the case), less satisfactory sources will have to be relied on.[1] The difficulties involved in preparing an unduplicated count of social service recipients vary widely among states. Some states have encountered problems in assimilating data on services purchased from other state agencies which have their own individual reporting systems. Other states have encountered issues of confidentiality in sensitive program areas, such as legal services and drug and alcohol abuse.[2] Furthermore, the current design of the federal social services reporting requirements (SSRR) means that variation is inherent in the interpretation and definition of "primary recipient."

For outcome monitoring purposes, a "perfect" list is not essential; what is required is a list that roughly covers the client categories of interest.

An interim approach would be to obtain client samples from each county office. This would require the participation of all county offices. Quality control of the sample drawing would be a problem, particularly in counties where records are not arranged conveniently. These and other options should be explored by states which intend to implement outcome-monitoring procedures.

A second issue in drawing the sample involves the obtaining of data on specific client groups. There appear to be two basic approaches: (1) stratify the population initially by various client categories and draw a sample

---

1. For example, North Carolina's "Daily Reports of Activity" forms are being used until its client tracking system is fully operational.

2. A few state officials have pointed out that there are difficulties involved in obtaining a list of service clients from local departments of social services. Most of these problems are technical, but a few may be organizational. Technical problems include situations in which case records are so bulky that the physical transfer of information would be prohibitively difficult (would require on-site visits to each county). Further, for some services (especially those provided without regard to income), case record documentation may not be available. While most states either have already developed a means of preparing unduplicated counts or have been making good faith efforts to do so, the Social and Rehabilitation Service of the U.S. Department of Health, Education and Welfare recently abolished its requirement for an unduplicated count. Although still encouraged to develop actual counts, states are now permitted to prepare "estimates." Organizational obstacles to the transmission of client data arise in the one-third of the states where the social service programs are locally administered. It appears, however, that the designated state agency for Title XX has the legal right to collect such information. (Information from the national survey of the client impact of social services by the Social and Rehabilitation Service of the U.S. Department of Health, Education and Welfare; this work is being done in preparation for a forthcoming report to Congress on Title XX.)

for each category, or (2) draw a random sample of all clients and hope that the size of each category is large enough to permit conclusions about outcomes for individual client groups.

A random sample of all clients would probably be the easiest procedure. It has the additional important advantage that the number drawn for each group would permit statistical estimates of the percentage of the total population that falls into each category. To stratify the sample would probably entail the need to examine numerous records in order to identify clients with the desired characteristics. Moreover, calculating statewide totals using stratified samples would entail separate estimates of the proportion of the total population that each stratum comprises.

On the other hand, a "simple" random sample could lead to undersampling some client groups and to oversampling others. A compromise might be to draw a much larger sample initially than is required. This large sample would provide data on the distribution of client characteristics in the population, and it would, if large enough, provide adequate sample sizes for even those client groupings with small populations. For client groups with samples larger than needed, client names could be randomly selected for deletion.[1] The drawback of this "large sample" option is that examination of client records is necessary before the final reduced sample is selected.

Each state should estimate how many clients in a random sample of a particular size would be likely to fall into each client group for which it wishes to obtain outcome data (for example, what percentage of clients would fall into each goal category, into each region of the state, into each type of program, and into each age, race, and income category, and so on). A test sampling of clients might be appropriate to obtain such estimates. This would provide an indication as to whether obtaining the required sample sizes will be a problem.[2] If it is found that a random sample would give adequate and rougly balanced sample sizes for most of the client groupings desired, the easier procedure of drawing a random sample from the total list would be justified.

3. When should the information be obtained on each client?

There are several interrelated issues here: (a) Should status at intake be assessed? (b) If so, for all clients or only for a sample? (c) If the

---

1. Note, however, that each client may have several characteristics, each of which is of interest. Thus, deleting clients from the sample may reduce sample size for other client groupings and put them below minimum desired sample sizes. The state should be careful that the remaining sample provides the desired minimum sample size for each category of interest.

2. The test would also provide an indication of the extent to which clients have multiple problems, have multiple goals, and have been provided multiple services. The estimation of the frequency with which clients are provided multiple services will also indicate the possibility of subsequent difficulties in relating outcome information to specific programs. The latter task would be more difficult if a large proportion of clients receive multiple services.

latter, should "cross-sectional" or "cohort" analysis be used? (d) Should the follow-up interval be related to the time of intake or to the time of exit from the program, and how long should the interval be before follow-up?

In order to obtain information on client change it is necessary to collect information on client condition at or near intake so that it can later be compared to client condition after services have been provided. Should information on condition at intake be collected from all incoming clients, or only from a sample? The former seems excessively expensive unless the information can be used operationally, such as by caseworkers for diagnostic purposes. The information gathered at intake for this assessment might ultimately prove useful to county offices, but it would be highly optimistic to assume that all or even most county offices will initially wish to add or substitute this new questionnaire for already existing forms.

If the decision is to use a sample, should the same clients be followed up to determine their improvement ("cohort" analysis), or should another sample of clients be taken at follow-up, with their condition compared with the condition of the clients assessed at intake ("cross-sectional" analysis)? For example, cross-sectional analysis might reveal that 36 percent of the clients tested at intake were unemployed and 25 percent of those tested at follow-up were unemployed. But this cross-sectional analysis would not indicate, for example, how many clients had moved from unemployed to employed status or how many had become unemployed since becoming clients.

The outcome information obtainable from these alternative approaches may be illustrated as follows:

1. If information on client condition is obtained only at follow-up, the outcome indicator would be the "percentage of clients at follow-up at each level of functioning."

2. If information is obtained at intake for one sample of clients and at follow-up for a different sample (but still drawn from the same group of clients), the outcome indicator would be the "percentage improvement in average scores."

3. If information is obtained for the same sample at both intake and follow-up, the outcome indicator would be the "percentage of clients improved."

Following the same clients has the advantage of reducing the sampling effects involved in comparing two different samples, but it also can pose a problem. Clients identified at intake as being members of the sample to be followed up may receive special attention that can invalidate the representativeness of the findings. To reduce this possibility, information obtained from clients at intake might be retained separately by the evaluation office and the clients' participation in the sample not indicated in the caseworkers' folders.[1]

The second issue is the timing of the follow-up interview. Although some fixed interval seems necessary to assure a common basis for comparing outcomes for different clients, several questions arise. How long should the interval be, and should it be linked to the time of entry or exit? Should it be linked to the time of entry (or termination) of each particular service or of only one service, such as the first or last service?

Choosing intake as the reference point has the advantage that follow-up can be scheduled at entry, with a "tickler" file to make sure the follow-up is undertaken on schedule. It also maximizes the likelihood that every client will be included in the population of clients to be sampled. Furthermore, the same length of time would be considered in each client's case, thus tending to permit fairer comparisons of results. It should be noted, however, that at the time of follow-up some clients will still be receiving services while others will have terminated. Moreover, different client problems are likely to require different time periods before significant improvements can be expected. These facts tend to make the interpretation of outcome data more difficult.

Alternatively, follow-up might be conducted at case closure, an option often suggested. Doing so, however, greatly limits the meaningfulness of follow-up information, especially for determining the extent to which self-sufficiency or self-support has been achieved. Many social services are intended to help the client become self-sufficient and self-supporting without further need for social services. Follow-up only at case closure would not provide meaningful evidence as to whether clients maintained any gains achieved.

Ideally, follow-up would be undertaken at some interval--such as six months or one year--after case closure. In conceptual terms, this approach would be the most effective in determining client success following services. It has some important practical problems, however:

1. Finding clients after closure is difficult and can become expensive, especially as the time after case closure lengthens.

2. It is probably more difficult procedurally to keep track of case closure dates than entry dates. This problem is exacerbated by differing definitions of case "closure" and differing applications of those definitions among local agency personnel.

---

1. Even this procedure might not prevent bias, since clients might tell their caseworkers that they have been interviewed for the study. The problem would not occur at all, however, if all clients were assessed at intake and the follow-up sample were drawn at the later date. Another option is to administer the questionnaire to more than the sample to be followed, thus preventing others from knowing which clients were in the follow-up sample.

3. Services for clients with continual difficulties may stretch out for long periods of time, thus tending to exclude such clients from the sample and potentially biasing the findings through exclusion of "difficult" cases.

What should be the time interval (after intake or case closure) before follow-up is made? There appears to be little current evidence to provide much guidance on this question. The time should be long enough to assure that outcomes represent more than temporary effects. Very early assessments are likely to be premature. On the other hand, in order for information to be meaningful to policy officials, outcome information should be available within a reasonable amount of time so that it can be related to current programs and policies. The longer the time period the more likely it is that external events not related to social services will affect the clients' status, and the more difficult and more expensive it will be to locate clients for follow-up. There is not much evidence available on the extent to which ability to locate ex-clients decreases as time beyond closure increases.

All in all, intervals of from six to twelve months after entry appear to be the principal candidates for time of follow-up. These same follow-up intervals also are candidates if referenced to the date of case closure.[1]

Another possibility is to group types of social service clients according to amount of time spent in the social service system and use different follow-up intervals for each group. The length of the interval, if referenced to the time of intake, could in part be determined by examining the distribution of clients with regard to time spent in the social service system. States could determine what proportion of various types of clients received social services for what length of time before determining the appropriate time interval for a follow-up. For example, in one county in the metropolitan Washington, D.C., area, approximately half of the clients had their cases closed within a thirty-day period, while clients receiving certain adult services (including aged persons) tended to stay in the social service system for an average of one to two years. In this same county foster care clients (including institutionalized children) averaged about two years, while family service cases averaged one year or so. Institutionalized adults (only 2 to 5 percent of the total clients of this county) received social services only when they were being committed to an institution or leaving it.[2]

A related problem is the possibility that a client may be involved with several services simultaneously or consecutively during the period of interest. Should clients be included again in the population to be sampled if they start

---

1. It should be recognized, however, that periodic special in-depth evaluations that follow clients for a longer period of time (to measure the long-term impact of state-supported services) are also highly desirable.

2. The extent to which institutionalized clients fall under Title XX is not clear. Inasmuch as Goal 5 explicitly mentions them--and social services can, of course, be defined so as not to be limited to Title XX services-- institutionalized clients have been considered as social service clients in these procedures.

a new program or a new goal? Or should clients be sampled only when they have
completed all goals or have terminated, without completion, all services?
Since the outcome measurement procedures discussed in this report focus on
the client rather than the specific service, it appears appropriate to time
the follow-up--if the reference point for the follow-up is the time of entry--
to the client's first entry rather than later entries into additional services.
If the reference point for the follow-up is the time of case closure, the closure of the client's last program would appear to be the appropriate reference
point. A drawback to waiting until all services or all goals are completed
is that this may mean prolonged "treatment" periods before a client's progress
is assessed. This will not be a serious problem, however, if the decision is
that only clients leaving the social service system will be included in outcome measurement. Putting clients into the list to be sampled after each
service is completed means that successes claimed by the delivery agency can
be checked in the follow-up survey.

There seems to be no perfect solution. A reasonable compromise is to
assess clients at intake and again one year after entry--with "entry" defined
as the time the first service is provided. Clients returning to social services after terminating all services would be included again in the population
from which subsequent years' samples would be drawn. (It is thus possible
that some persons would be sampled more than once.) The "change measure" that
would be obtained would be the "percentage of clients who showed various degrees of improvement one year after entry." During each year a new sample
would be selected from cases opened at various times throughout the year and
the clients followed up twelve months after entry. This procedure requires
interviewing to be conducted on a year-round basis.[1]

4. Who should administer the questionnaire?

Some of the data on client conditions can be obtained from government
records. However, much of the information identified in Chapter 1 requires an
interview with the client. The information would probably be best obtained
by independent experienced interviewers, but this practice may be too expensive for some governments. At intake, the information might instead be
obtained by the intake worker. In general, however, in order to avoid possible
bias and ensuing credibility problems a client's own caseworker should not do
the follow-up. Having employees in effect evaluate their own work is not
generally believed to provide the most accurate data, and the information
would probably be suspect.[2] There are also other problems. Using caseworkers

---

1. A less desirable alternative would be to conduct the intake and follow-
up interviews during a selected period of each year, such as the three summer
months each year. This scheme could, however, result in seasonal biases and
might not be representative of the full year's clients.

2. A recent study for the Social and Rehabilitation Service of the U.S.
Department of Health, Education and Welfare presented data from the states of
Maine and Iowa that compared caseworker ratings of outcome on attaining self-
support to "objective" data on employment status. There were major discrep-
ancies between the two sets of ratings. For example, for 1,297 clients
(56 percent of the 2,300 cases examined), caseworkers had indicated "goal
achieved," but the clients were "unemployed, available for work." Note,
however, that this was not a test of a situation in which caseworkers used
a standardized set of definitions of "goal achieved." U.S. Department of
Health, Education and Welfare, Social and Rehabilitation Service, Social
Services Effectiveness Study: A "Service-Generic" Evaluation of the Effectiveness of Social Services (1976), p. 35.

is likely to overload them with work, especially if the interviews are conducted after clients have left the system. In addition, it will probably be very difficult to maintain quality control over the several hundred caseworkers who would have to be trained.

Instead, a relatively small number of trained interviewers should probably be used. These could either be state personnel or persons on contract from a local university or survey research organization. To save out-of-pocket funds a government is likely to want to use in-house personnel. This is acceptable if such persons are properly trained for the interviews and their work is monitored as to quality. Unless there is a permanent in-house staff capable of conducting interviews, however, the contract approach has the advantage of relieving the state agency of many administrative headaches, such as obtaining the personnel to undertake the interviews when needed, providing their training, and monitoring the quality. If a state agency decides to do these tasks in-house, at the very least a survey specialist should be present to participate in the training of personnel and monitor the conduct of the survey. The interviewers need not have a social work background. All that seems necessary is good interviewer training, perhaps with the help of social service personnel. The state of Minnesota, for example, is considering using county representatives, whose responsibilities include evaluation, to conduct such follow-up interviews.

5. How should the interviews be undertaken?

Should they be conducted by mail, by telephone, in person, or by some combination of all three? Cost increases considerably from mail to telephone to in-person interviewing. The last is the most expensive because of transportation costs (although some intake interviews may be conducted when clients are in the agency for regular appointments). Both telephone interviewing and in-person interviewing require trained interviewers and effort to try to reach persons in the sample. A mail survey has major problems because of its typically low response rate, the need to keep the mail questionnaire short (so that clients will be more likely to respond), and the inherent limitations of written questions. Telephone or in-person interviewing, or some combination of all three modes, appears to be most suitable. But the mail approach (which has been used for some mental health client follow-ups) is not completely out of the question if telephone or in-person interviews are also used for clients who do not respond by mail. A shortened form of the questionnaire shown in Appendix A would probably be needed for a mail survey in order to assure reasonable response rates.[1]

In order for the findings to be representative of the full social service clientele, the sample should contain as high a percentage as possible of those whose names have been drawn. Thus, the ability of the state to locate ex-clients for follow-up becomes critical. The state of Maine's 1973 experience suggests

---

1. The state of Missouri, using two mail-outs (two weeks apart) of the questionnaire at intake to relatives and friends of the clients, obtained a response rate of approximately 70 percent.

that substantial difficulties may occur.[1] Any state intending to conduct a follow-up study should consider procedures to maximize the response rate, such as (1) advance letters to ex-clients asking for their cooperation and allowing them to specify a convenient time for the interview, (2) multiple mailings or call-backs, (3) obtaining from clients at intake and exit the names, addresses, and telephone numbers of relatives or acquaintances who could specify their whereabouts, and (4) the use of experienced interviewers to deal with ex-clients who initially refuse to be interviewed. If in-person interviews are used, mail and telephone can be used to help locate clients so that costs are reduced.

Our current recommendation is to test the use of telephone interviewing where telephone numbers are available, with at-home interviews used where numbers are not available but an address is.

6. How can the "confidentiality and privacy" issues be properly handled?

An overriding concern is to maintain the confidentiality of information given by individual clients and ex-clients. Outcome information is intended to be used only in aggregate forms, for statistical purposes, and should not be incorporated into individual case files. Findings on individual clients should not be reported. However, those involved in the outcome monitoring procedures--including, of course, interviewers and those initially processing the data--will need access to information on the individual clients sampled. The cooperation of clients, especially ex-clients, can only be voluntary. Social service departments should obtain the written agreement of clients to participate in a follow-up study. But participation, of course, cannot be required.[2]

All persons involved in follow-up surveys should be made aware of their responsibility to keep information confidential. The follow-up information form should have client identification removed after it is no longer needed. In any case, it is incumbent on the state to establish procedures that protect the confidentiality of clients.

---

1. Maine reported the following: Of about 2,440 clients chosen at random (this sample included both open and closed cases of various lengths), in-person interviews were completed with 53 percent. About 13 percent had moved out of the state or had left no forwarding address; another 13 percent refused to be interviewed or failed to keep two appointments; 14 percent were not located; about 2 percent were deceased; 2 percent were institutionalized clients who could not respond and for whom surrogate respondents were not available; and about 3 percent claimed not to have been served. (See Volume II for more details.)

2. See the appendix in Volume II of this book for an illustrative "consent form" used by the Denver Community Mental Health team in their client follow-up work.

Chapter 4

SUGGESTIONS FOR THE VALIDATION OF CLIENT OUTCOME-MONITORING PROCEDURES

There has been little testing of social service outcome-monitoring procedures either in this effort or by others. Most of what has been done has
been in the form of special studies on specific client groups. Additional
testing and validation is needed whenever a new instrument or procedure is
being considered for use, even though it is based partly on prior efforts (as
is the case with the procedures presented here).

What follows are a number of validation steps that should be considered
by governments planning to implement outcome-monitoring procedures such as
those proposed in this report.

1. At the very least, considerable effort should be directed toward <u>face
validation</u> of the questionnaire. Does the information sought by the questionnaire seem, on the face of it, likely to assess client conditions that are
related to the outcomes of state social services? Each question should elicit
relevant information. In addition, the questionnaire, considered as a whole,
should cover a significant part of the outcomes of state social services. Each
question should (a) provide information directly on a desired outcome such as
information on a person's ability to function in a specific activity; or
(b) be a part of a series of questions that together provide the information
noted in (a); or (c) provide "explanatory" or descriptive information that will
be useful in analyzing the findings. Inasmuch as each government will have
its own conceptions of outcomes desired as a result of its social service programs, it is necessary for each to determine face validity for itself. Persons
from various levels of government and various service delivery agencies should
participate in this review.

2. The questionnaire should be pretested through actual interviews with
at least a small number of clients.[1] It is important to include some of each
of the main categories of clients in the pretest so that the applicability

---

1. A questionnaire similar to that shown in Appendix A was pretested in
September–October 1976 in two North Carolina counties with thirty-five current
and four ex-clients. The pretest interviews were conducted by nine members
of the North Carolina Department of Human Resources (Social Services and
Evaluation Divisions) and one member of The Urban Institute.

of the instrument to the clients can be determined. (It is likely that each
state will want to focus on selected categories of clients, such as neglected
children, adults with limited economic means and other selected problems,
and disabled aged clients.) The sample in the pretest should include
(a) clients at intake, to pretest the intake version of the instrument, and
(b) clients who have terminated services, as well as some that have not yet
terminated, to pretest the follow-up version.

A major function of the pretest is to ascertain whether each question
elicits the information it purports to assess, and whether each question is
as clear and unambiguous as possible. One way to identify problems is to
ask respondents why a particular response was given. For example, the interviewer might ask the respondent, "Why did you say that?" when the respondent
rates some aspect (such as waiting time) of the services provided. Interviewers should try to determine whether respondents are indeed considering
the issue that is to be addressed. This is especially important when questions, such as those concerning family strength, are conceptually complex.
For example, if respondents state that they had problems with their spouses,
it may be useful to ask "What kind of problems?" in order to determine
whether the responses have to do with interpersonal relationships or something
else, such as "My spouse is ill and in the hospital."

3. For questions that are important but difficult to phrase, the evaluation team should consider including in the pretest similar, overlapping questions in different parts of the questionnaire or differently worded versions
of the same question. In either case the purpose is to see if one form appears
more appropriate than the other. To do this would require questioning the
respondent to determine whether each particular form was clearly understood.
When two similar questions elicit consistent responses, either is likely to be
suitable. (It may also be appropriate in a few instances to leave redundant
questions in the final questionnaire to permit evaluators to make consistency
checks.)

4. The interviewers in the pretest should discuss with the evaluation
team their judgments as to whether the questions seemed understandable to
respondents and the answers reasonable. In addition, interviewers can provide
valuable insight into the appropriateness of various sets of questions for
various types of clients and various client situations. The pretest can also
test the adequacy of interviewer training if some of the interviewers in the
pretest are the same as those intended for actual implementation. Hence, as
part of the pretest, the type of interviewers (in-house or contract) and the
amount of training provided (which should be documented) could be tested.

5. Special attention should be paid during the pretest to cases involving
respondents who do not complete interviews, in order to determine the nature of
problems that may have arisen. In addition, the evaluating team should examine
those situations involving clients who were not located. The characteristics

of clients who could not be located, or who did not give complete interviews although they were located, should be examined to see if something unusual happened. Special efforts may be appropriate to locate and interview at least a subsample of such persons in order to determine whether their responses differ significantly from the responses of other clients. This would also provide data on the extra effort and cost required to locate hard-to-find clients.

6. For those (few) questions that address factual information (such as employment and income data), responses to the pretest might be checked by examining other sources (for example, unemployment compensation records or state income tax information). Such checking is not likely to be possible in many instances, but it does provide an effective validation technique when available.

7. Reinterviews of a few clients by different interviewers in the pretest might be undertaken. Significant differences in ratings between interviews would be cause for concern and would require careful analysis to correct possible problems. Differences might be due to interviewer problems, question-wording problems, or to respondents' uncooperativeness. (This may be one of the few tests available for questions on client satisfaction, which otherwise are nearly impossible to validate directly.) These reinterviews should be undertaken within a short time (a few days) to minimize the likelihood that a real change has taken place.

8. Another validation technique is to interview relatives or friends of clients and compare their responses with those of the clients. This would, of course, require the permission of the clients.

9. When clients are still receiving services at the time of the pretest follow-up interviews, or have very recently completed services, it may be useful to compare their responses with independent ratings by the clients' own caseworkers. (Note that this is suggested only for validation studies.) Another option is to compare the findings from the interview with those obtained from a caseworker who does not know the client. The caseworker would make an independent examination of case records and perhaps interview the client, but not using the client outcome questionnaire. Major differences between the client's and caseworker's ratings should be examined to determine whether there are procedural problems and how they might be corrected.

10. Once the elements of the questionnaire are made final, the scoring technique (see Chapter 2) should be assessed. To do this, a group of "experts" could independently provide overall ratings for each dimension or indicator. These would then be compared with the dimension or indicator rating obtained from the scoring procedure. On the assumption that the experts' overall ratings are likely to be "good" ones, a scoring technique that provided ratings similar to those of the experts would be considered acceptable.

11. A highly useful approach is to compare, for selected dimensions or indicators, the scores of clients known to have particular problems with the scores of a sample of the general community. This was done by the developers

of the Denver Community Mental Health Questionnaire for the questions that
have subsequently been adapted by us for use in determining Indicator 10,
index of mental distress. The test here is to see if the scoring procedures
provide scores that can distinguish clients known to have a problem from the
general public.

12. Another test is to compare the scores of a sample of clients with
their characteristics as measured by other indicators known to be highly
correlated with the behavior the questions are attempting to assess. For
example, Lawton and Brody compared ratings obtained by using scales measuring activities of daily living with scores from three other scales which pur-
ported to assess similar items and on which previous validation work had
been done.[1] A problem with this test is the paucity of well-tested and well-
validated scales for comparison.

With any of the above validation efforts, attempts should be made to
resolve any problems found. If these problems require major changes, additional pretesting may be needed. This point may seem obvious, but in the
usual rush to meet implementation deadlines testing of corrective actions is
often the first thing to be dropped.

An important element in maintaining the validity of outcome-monitoring
information is care in undertaking the various procedures: obtaining reasonably complete lists of clients from which samples are to be drawn, drawing
the samples properly, obtaining reasonable response rates from those drawn
in the sample, interviewing properly, and processing and tallying results
accurately.

Until at least some such testing has been successfully undertaken, a
government cannot be reasonably confident about the ability of the questionnaire and procedures to elicit accurately the kind of information the state
seeks.

---

1. Lawton and Brody, "Assessment of Older People."

Chapter 5

ESTIMATING UNMET NEED

The preceding chapters dealt with the outcomes of social services for clients. It is important to recognize, however, that there may be many citizens who have not become clients but who need services. An estimate of "unmet need" in the general population would provide both an indication of the extent to which social services are reaching those in need and information useful for considering changes in service priorities and distribution.

Unmet need for social services can be estimated, at least roughly, by means of state (or community) sample surveys. Other methods have also been used, such as statistical projections based on census data and surveys of social service professionals and other knowledgeable groups. This chapter discusses a general citizen survey approach, designed to be used either by itself or in conjunction with other needs assessment methodologies.

Conceptual Framework and Suggested Approach

Surveys used to assess unmet need for social services generally utilize one or both of these basic methods:

(1) They collect data on various "conditions"--such as low income, advanced age or illness, and disability--which are believed to define groups of citizens who are "at risk" for certain problems and therefore may be in need of certain services.

(2) They ask survey respondents for their subjective opinions as to whether they have certain problems or need certain services.

The "citizen conditions" approach may seem more objective, but need cannot usually be inferred solely from this information. For example, data on the incidence of blindness does not measure the extent of unmet need for services for the blind because many blind persons either need no social services or already receive them. To accurately measure "objectively" the incidence of problems or combinations of problems which imply needs for specific services, it is necessary to develop a way to define such problems by the symptoms or conditions experienced. Problems for which social services are needed are often complex and not easily defined. An extensive amount of questioning would be necessary to achieve a degree of detail

adequate for inferring actual needs for services from "conditions."[1] This
approach may be too cumbersome and expensive for a general citizen survey
covering all social services. Therefore the emphasis here is on the second
approach--asking survey respondents for their perceptions of whether they
have various problems and needs for service. (A jurisdiction with sufficient
money and time, however, might try a combination of these approaches.)

Except for involuntary services (such as child protective services and
involuntary commitment for psychiatric or medical conditions), a person's
awareness of, and willingness to admit to, having a "problem" is usually a
prerequisite for seeking social services. Therefore a question which asks
for a respondent's perception of whether he or she has a problem will probably
tend to identify most of the persons who might use social services in the
immediate future. This approach, however, will fail to identify citizens
who have problems but do not perceive, or will not admit, that they have them.[2]

The operating definition of unmet need used here is as follows:

(a) The respondent perceives himself or herself (or another household
     member) as having a given problem and perceives the problem to
     be one for which he or she (or other household member) needs or
     wishes help, but

(b) The respondent (or other household member) has not sought help, or

(c) The respondent (or other household member), though seeking help,
     has not received it.

Appendix B presents an illustrative questionnaire designed to estimate
"unmet need" as defined above. For each social-service-related problem area,
respondents are asked:

(1) Whether (in the past year) they felt that someone in their household
     had the problem;

(2) If so, how important the problem was;

---

1. See Volume II of this report for further discussion of this issue and
reviews of other needs assessment studies. When a survey collects data on
"social conditions" and "symptoms" experienced by citizens, rather than asking
directly for their perceptions of their needs, the analysis must include a
procedure for deriving "needs" from conditions and symptoms data. In order to
develop this procedure, the analysts must identify what symptoms and conditions
comprise each "need." The procedure for defining need should be systematically
developed and tested, rather than resting on untested assumptions about the
needs of persons with various conditions. Although there have been many
studies which collected "conditions" data, the validity of their procedures
for deriving "needs" from the data does not appear to have been confirmed.

2. If a social service system has as a major goal the education of
citizens to be more aware of their problems and to be more willing to consider getting help with them, it would be important to try to overcome the
difficulties involved in detecting persons with problems who are unaware of
them. Such a goal is not now a priority for social service systems, which
are often overwhelmed by the current demands for services.

(3)   Whether help was sought, and if not, why not; and

(4)   If help was sought, whether help was received, and if not, why not.[1]

The answers to this series of questions provide estimates of the "percentage of respondents who felt that someone in their household had a social-service-related problem, but did not seek help, for reasons that the government could have influenced"(queries 1, 2, and 3), and the "percentage of respondents who reported that help was sought but not received, for reasons that the government could have influenced" (query 4). These two measures can then be combined to provide the "percentage of respondents indicating that someone in their household had an unmet need for help with at least one social-service-related problem" (Indicator 30 in Exhibit 1). Exhibit 3 divides this indicator into problem areas and lists the appropriate survey questions from Appendix B.

A key concern is the accurate identification of reasons for not seeking help and for not receiving help when it was sought, particularly those reasons that the government is likely to be able to do something about. (An initial set of reasons that might be used is shown in Appendix B in the "answer module" on page B-3.) Reasons relatively immune to government action include "could handle problem without help," "no one else could help," "didn't want to go to outsiders," "didn't want public help," and "too busy."[2] Reasons which the government may be able to influence include "thought no help was available," "couldn't afford help," "thought I wasn't eligible," "didn't know how to find help," "transportation problems," and "no one to temporarily care for children."

The ability and willingness of the respondent to respond accurately on these questions is, of course, of great importance. Intentional inaccuracies can be minimized through the use of proper interviewing procedures and well-trained, motivated interviewers. But unintentional errors can and will occur. Tests of the validity of information obtained from citizens on unmet needs are likely to be difficult and possibly quite expensive. In lieu of such testing, the questions should be examined by state agencies for face validity and pretested in order to achieve the best specific wording.

---

1. In addition to asking whether persons obtained help, the questionnaire proposed here also asks whether those who obtained services were satisfied, and if not, why not. However, it is likely that only a small number of respondents will have received services, so that this is not a good way to obtain client satisfaction ratings, especially as compared to the client outcome-monitoring procedures described earlier. In tabulating the data, users of the survey have a choice as to whether to include those who received services but were not satisfied among the "unmet need" group.

2. Any of these reasons, especially "didn't want public help," may indicate concern about a "stigma" attached both to admitting a need for help and to going to a public agency. In-depth exploration of all reasons for not seeking help would perhaps be worthwhile to learn more precisely how the state could assist those needing help in seeking it--to explore the gap between "need" and "demand."

EXHIBIT 3

INDICATORS OF UNMET NEED FOR SOCIAL SERVICES AND
SURVEY QUESTIONS FROM WHICH THE INDICATORS ARE DERIVED*

<u>Indicator</u>   Question**

1. Percentage of respondents who felt someone in their household had a <u>financial problem</u>, but either did not seek help, for reasons that the government could have influenced, or sought help and did not receive it, for reasons that the government could have influenced.   1

2. Percentage of respondents who felt that someone in their household had an <u>employment problem</u>, but . . .   2

3. Percentage of respondents who felt that someone in their household had <u>inadequate medical or dental care</u>, but . . .   3

4. Percentage of respondents who felt that someone in their household had <u>personal care (ADL) problems</u>, but . . .   4

5. Percentage of respondents who felt that someone in their household had <u>problems with care of a disabled family member</u>, but . . .   5

6. Percentage of respondents who felt that someone in their household was <u>unhappy with self or life situation</u>, but . . .   6

7. Percentage of respondents who felt that someone in their household was <u>mentally ill, retarded, or senile</u>, but . . .   7

8. Percentage of respondents who felt that someone in their household had <u>family problems</u>, but . . .   8

9. Percentage of respondents who felt that someone in their household had a <u>drinking problem</u>, but . . .   9

10. Percentage of respondents who felt that someone in their household had a <u>drug problem</u>, but . . .   10

11. Percentage of respondents who felt that someone in their household had a problem with <u>social isolation</u>, but . . .   11

12. Percentage of respondents who felt that someone in their household had <u>problems with children</u>, but . . .   12

13. Percentage of respondents who felt that someone in their household had <u>problems with day care of children</u>, but . . .   13

14. Percentage of respondents who felt that someone in their household had <u>family planning problems</u>, but . . .   14

15. Percentage of respondents who felt that someone in their household had <u>transportation problems</u>, but . . .   15

16. Percentage of respondents who felt that someone in their household had <u>housing problems</u>, but . . .   16

17. Percentage of respondents who felt that someone in their household had <u>problems other than those above</u>, but . . .   17

18. Percentage of respondents who felt that someone in their household had <u>at least one social-service-related problem</u>, but . . .   All of the above

*The indicators might also be broken down by severity, for example, "the percentage of respondents who felt that someone in their household had a <u>major</u> problem."
**See Appendix B.

Content of the Citizen Survey

Appendix B contains an illustrative brief set of questions intended to serve as a prototype for a general citizen survey to estimate unmet needs. The set is a synthesis of a number of needs surveys undertaken by various states, including Wisconsin's multiservice survey. The set of questions in Appendix B, however, has not itself been tested. The questions constitute a relatively compact needs-assessment package that can be administered either alone or as part of a multiservice citizen survey. It is estimated to require an average of about ten to fifteen minutes per interview.

There are two prime categories of questions needed for the survey: (1) demographic questions, and (2) needs questions.

Demographic questions. The demographic questions cover geographic location; racial or ethnic group; household composition by age, sex, and relationship; and household income group. These variables are important in the analysis of needs data and, because they may identify groups of citizens with high proportions of unmet needs, can be useful for planning the siting and staffing of services.

Needs questions. Each of the "needs" questions asks about a problem which may indicate a need for service and explores the respondent's experience and attitudes with regard to seeking and obtaining service. Exhibit 4 presents an illustrative list of problems included in the survey that may lead to needs for social services, matched with social services often offered in government programs. Some problems may be alleviated by several different services. The questionnaire is an attempt to cover these problems as comprehensively as possible without excessive repetition.

The needs questions focus on problems rather than on specific social services, on the assumptions that people seek help from many sources other than social service agencies and that many people do not know about some of the services which are available.[1] The questions are directed at problem areas rather than specific problems. Narrowing the focus to identify specific problems would require many more questions and would be more appropriate for special studies focusing on individual problem areas. The list of questions is designed to be short enough to use for regular (such as annual) monitoring of unmet need for all social services, perhaps as part of a larger statewide survey covering other service areas such as recreation and transportation.

The "answer module" used for the needs questions (see Appendix B) is designed to elicit information as to reasons why respondents who perceived they had a problem did not seek or did not find help. The questions proceed from asking about the existence of problems and their degrees of importance as citizens perceive them, to efforts to seek help. The questions on "reasons"

---

1. Several studies have found indications that these assumptions are correct. For example, the Florida survey of the elderly (described in Volume II) found data indicating lack of information about services and disinclination to seek public services for certain types of problems.

EXHIBIT 4

"PROBLEMS" TO BE COVERED IN NEEDS SURVEY AND
GOVERNMENT SERVICES WHICH MAY PROVIDE HELP FOR THEM

Problem	Service*
--Financial problems	Advocacy services to facilitate obtaining public financial aid Legal services to obtain child support, declare bankruptcy, and so forth **Counseling to help make decision on what action to take, mobilize activity **Information and referral services
--Employment problems	Job counseling Training or education Counseling, information and referral Legal services
--Medical/dental care inadequate	Advocacy Home medical care Counseling, information and referral Special transportation services, like ambulettes or cab fare for trips to clinics
--Disability (mental or physical) which seriously inhibits functioning and ability to perform activities of daily living; difficulties with caring for disabled persons	Homemaking, home health aide, chore services Visiting nurse Life skills education (training in ADL) Home delivered meals, group meal programs Adult day care, adult foster homes, group homes Institutional care
--Dissatisfaction with self, life, emotional problems short of diagnosed mental illness	Counseling, information and referral
--Mental illness, mental retardation, senility	Counseling, information and referral Adult day care Institutional care
--Family problems, marital conflict, disorganization	Counseling Homemaking
--Alcoholism, drug abuse	Information and referral to medical treatment, self-help groups, and so forth Residential treatment centers Counseling
--Social isolation	Counseling Senior centers, adult day care Friendly visiting, telephone reassurance Recreation services, adult camping
--Child problems, behavior problems, delinquency, child abuse and neglect, severe parent-child conflict, parent needs help with child care	Child protective services Child day care Family-life education Foster care, adoption, institutional care Camping Counseling, information and referral
--Family planning problems, wish to increase or limit family size, infertility	Family planning Adoption Counseling, information and referral
--Transportation problems, difficulty getting around because of disability, lack of car/bus service, money problems	Special transportation services, such as minibus routes for elderly, cab fare, ambulettes Counseling, information and referral
--Housing inadequate, in poor repair, neighborhood unsafe, other dissatisfactions	Housing assistance to find new housing, obtain repairs Legal services to obtain repairs, forestall eviction Counseling, information and referral

*This listing excludes direct financial services.

**For this and all other problems listed, counseling may be needed to help the person focus on a problem, decide what to do about it, and act. Information and referral services may be needed in many cases to help the person obtain other help with the problem. Legal services may also be required in many problem areas, such as for legal separation or divorce, protection of civil rights in commitments, and so forth.

may be asked as open-ended questions, or respondents might be asked specifically about each of the reasons, or both. If the first approach is used, interviewers should be trained to probe when necessary and to code responses. Open-ended questions have the advantage of minimizing "suggestions" to the respondent.

The questions in Appendix B ask the respondent about both the respondent's own problems and those of other members of the household. Asking about the entire household widens the coverage of the survey to include many more people, gives a better picture of household problems, and reduces the bias that might be present if it is true that family members who are interviewed are less likely to be those with problems. The disadvantage in asking a respondent about other household members is the respondent's lack of firsthand knowledge about other family members' problems and attitudes, especially on the key questions as to why the person did not seek or did not receive help.

There appears to be limited evidence as to the potential reliability of such information provided by a respondent on other household members. It would be desirable to test how accurately respondents are likely to respond for others, but this would require extensive efforts to interview other members after an initial respondent was interviewed.[1]

Administration of the Survey

It is crucial that the sample of citizens for the survey be selected scientifically to be sure that those surveyed are representative of the total population. Poor sampling techniques can destroy the value of the survey.

---

1. Some testing of the accuracy of "secondhand" information has been done for the nationwide Health Interview Survey (HIS). As expected, even for relatively factual data--reporting of episodes of hospitalization, injuries in motor vehicle accidents, and chronic health conditions--the HIS found that proxy responses (information given by persons other than those who were hospitalized, injured, or ill) were consistently and significantly less accurate than self-responses. Although the differences were small, total incidents were generally underestimated by proxy respondents. See: U.S. Department of Health, Education and Welfare, Public Health Service, "Quality Control and Measurement of Nonsampling Error in the Health Interview Survey," Vital and Health Statistics, series 2, no. 54, pp. 20-21; "Reporting of Hospitalization in the Health Interview Survey," Vital and Health Statistics, series 2, no. 6, pp. 14-15; and "Optimum Recall Period for Reporting Persons Injured in Motor Vehicle Accidents," Vital and Health Statistics, series 2, no. 50, pp. 6-7. However, for a general survey of the type proposed here-- where no attempt is made to define problems in detail--small differences in accuracy of responses may be less important than broadening the coverage of the survey to include entire households.

The questionnaire may be administered in person, or by telephone, by an experienced interviewer. Social work background does not appear to be necessary for the interviewer. A university or private survey firm is likely to be adequate; however, some studies have found that the use of professional social workers as interviewers results in findings of higher incidences of certain problems--for example, marital conflict--than similar studies using nonprofessional interviewers.

It is beyond the scope of this report to discuss citizen survey procedures; there are texts already available on this topic.[1]

Cost of the Survey

In two Florida needs-assessment surveys reviewed in Volume II the cost of interviews averaged $20 apiece for in-person interviews using much longer questionnaires than the one in Appendix B. New Jersey contracted for over 3,000 interviews similar in length to the one presented here; the state paid approximately $48,000 for the interviews and for data analysis. The states of North Carolina and Wisconsin each contracted for thirty-minute multiple-service citizen surveys of 1,500 and 2,000 households, respectively, for approximately $15 each, about $25,000 to 30,000 total. These costs included pretesting, telephone interviewing, coding, and basic tabulations, but did not include constructing a questionnaire from "scratch" or in-depth analysis of the survey findings.

Analysis and Utilization of Survey Results

The data collected by the survey can be analyzed to provide a set of indicators of unmet need for social services. Exhibits 5 and 6 provide illustrations of formats that might be used to present the types of data provided by the survey. Exhibit 5 presents the indicators for the problems that respondents might be queried about. Exhibit 6 illustrates how the data might be summarized to show the findings for one problem area for various client groups. To identify population subgroups having relatively high proportions of unmet need in the various problem areas, cross-tabulations should be done with the various demographic variables.

Among the ways the findings may be used are:

(1) To identify for program planners the problems that are generating high levels of unmet need (special studies can then be done to define further the problems and service needs).

---

1. For discussion of survey methodology, see: Carol H. Weiss and Harry P. Hatry, An Introduction to Sample Surveys for Government Managers (Washington, D.C.: The Urban Institute, 1971); Morris J. Slonim, Sampling in a Nutshell (New York: Simon and Schuster, 1960); Earl R. Babbie, Survey Research Methods (Belmont, California: Wadsworth Publishing Co., 1973); and U.S. Executive Office of the President, Bureau of the Budget, Household Survey Manual, 1969 (Washington, D.C., 1970).

EXHIBIT 5

ILLUSTRATIVE DISPLAY FORMAT FOR SUMMARIZING DATA
ON UNMET NEEDS: BY TYPE OF PROBLEM

TYPE OF PROBLEM	Percentage of respondents who had the problem but <u>did not seek help</u>, for reasons that the government could have influenced	+ Percentage of respondents who had the problem and sought but <u>did not get help</u>, for reasons that the government could have influenced	= Percentage of respondents indicating that they had unmet need for social services
FINANCIAL			
EMPLOYMENT			
MEDICAL/DENTAL			
PERSONAL CARE			
CARING FOR DISABLED FAMILY MEMBER			
DISSATISFACTION WITH SELF, LIFE			
MENTAL ILLNESS, RETARDATION, SENILITY			
FAMILY PROBLEMS			
DRINKING PROBLEM			
DRUG PROBLEM			
SOCIAL ISOLATION			
PROBLEMS WITH CHILDREN			
NEED DAY CARE FOR CHILDREN			
FAMILY PLANNING			
TRANSPORTATION			
HOUSING			
OTHER			
<u>TOTAL</u>: RESPONDENTS WITH AT LEAST ONE PROBLEM			

NOTE: These indicators should be obtained for specific population groups, such as those living in various parts of the state, or those of different ages, incomes, or racial or ethnic groups.

EXHIBIT 6

ILLUSTRATIVE FORMAT FOR SUMMARIZING CITIZEN SURVEY DATA ON UNMET NEEDS BY CLIENT GROUP*

Problem Area:
_____

	Reasons for Not Seeking Help							Reasons for Not Getting Help						
	Thought no help was available	Thought couldn't afford help	Thought not eligible	Didn't know how to find help	Transportation problem	No one to care for child/other family member temporarily	TOTAL PERCENTAGE OF RESPONDENTS WHO HAD PROBLEM BUT DID NOT SEEK HELP, FOR REASONS THAT THE GOVERNMENT COULD HAVE INFLUENCED	Couldn't find help	Couldn't afford help	Not eligible	Transportation problem	No one to care for child/other family member temporarily	TOTAL PERCENTAGE OF RESPONDENTS WHO HAD PROBLEM AND SOUGHT BUT DID NOT GET HELP, FOR REASONS THAT THE GOVERNMENT COULD HAVE INFLUENCED	TOTAL PERCENTAGE OF RESPONDENTS WITH UNMET NEED
Number responding														
Percentage of total responding														
Respondent Class	Percentage of Respondents in Class													
Sex and Race: White male														
White female														
Nonwhite male														
Nonwhite female														
Age: 18-34														
35-49														
50-64														
65 and over														
Family Income: Under $3,000														
$3,000-4,999														
$5,000-7,999														
$8,000-9,999														
$10,000-15,000														
Over $15,000														
Region: 1. Central														
2. Northeast														
3. Northwest														
4. Southeast														
5. Southwest														

*A table like this could be provided for each problem area (see Exhibit 3).

(2) To identify population subgroups that appear to have high
    levels of unmet need.

(3) To indicate where improvements in service delivery are needed
    in order to minimize difficulties that prevent citizens from
    seeking or obtaining help.

If the survey is conducted regularly--for example, annually--it will
indicate the extent to which citizen problems and unmet needs have changed
over time. This information can be used as an important indicator of outcomes of state provision of social services--the extent to which the government is meeting the needs of citizens under its jurisdiction. However,
because external factors--economic recessions, natural disasters, and the
like--also influence unmet need in the population, and because many services
are delivered by nonstate sources, a cause-and-effect relationship cannot
be inferred.

Chapter 6

THE UTILIZATION OF OUTCOME-MONITORING INFORMATION

This chapter discusses three aspects of the use of outcome data: (1) the various uses for the data themselves; (2) methods for reporting such data in order to facilitate their use; and (3) ways to analyze the data.

Because of the current limited availability of outcome information, there is little specific experience to draw on in discussing these issues. The following are preliminary suggestions, based whenever possible on actual government experiences.

Uses for Outcome Monitoring Data

In this section, a number of uses for outcome measurement information are discussed: (1) review of progress and trends of social services; (2) resource allocation decisions; (3) budget formulation and justification; (4) in-depth program evaluation and program analysis; (5) employee motivation; (6) performance contracting; (7) quality control checks on efficiency measurements; (8) improved communication of citizens and clients with government officials; and (9) local management control (a potential future use).

1. Review of progress and trends of social services. If data collection procedures such as those described in this report are undertaken regularly, performance can be reviewed and compared from year to year. This will permit identification of problem areas, of progress that has been made, and, after several years of data collection, time trends. (However, any problems that are identified will require closer study in order to determine what actions are needed.) Progress and time trends can indicate to government officials whether services are being adequately provided, particularly after major program changes are implemented.

2. Resource allocation decisions. By identifying problem areas, outcome information can help provide guidance to social service managers and central management on the allocation of resources. In particular, if the measurement data are segregated by geographical area and major client group (as suggested throughout this report), they will indicate which specific geographical areas and client groups appear to have greater problems or needs than others. The use of outcome information to help determine the allocation of resources is a significant move away from "squeaky wheel" decision-making.

Information on "unmet needs" (see Chapter 5), as the term implies, can be used by governments to estimate the approximate magnitude of unmet needs by geographic area, and this information can be used to help justify budget proposals.

It is important to note, however, that because of probable restrictions on sample sizes (due to limited evaluation funds) in both client outcome-monitoring efforts and unmet needs surveys, the findings are not likely to be appropriate for helping to make resource allocations among specific counties or within individual counties. Only if individual county agencies are able to supplement state sample sizes with large enough samples of their own will the findings be helpful in internal county resource allocation decisions.

Some resource allocation decisions involve the budgetary process, while others do not. Because of the importance of the budgetary process, it is discussed separately in the next section.

3. Budget formulation and justification. The budgetary process is a major element in the resource allocation activities of government. Information obtained from regular monitoring of social service outcomes should be formally incorporated into the budgetary process, with provision for obtaining the information at a time that fits conveniently into a jurisdiction's budget cycle. After outcome-monitoring procedures have been tested and appear to be reliable, the information obtained can become an element of budget preparation and justification. Such information should help guide initial budget decisions and should subsequently help government officials provide better justifications to the legislature and to the public. Jurisdictions with some form of program budgeting, zero-base budgeting, planning-programming-budgeting system, or the like should find outcome information very useful in rationalizing budget choices. Without the regular availability of information about the effectiveness of individual government services, it is hard to see how such budgeting procedures, or variations thereof, can be truly meaningful.[1]

4. In-depth program evaluation and program analysis. Examining the performance of existing programs (program evaluation) and considering various options for future implementation (program analysis) are basic elements of management. Some agencies responsible for social services have begun to make provision, sometimes with separate staffs, for undertaking in-depth studies on major program issues. These efforts include the collection of information relating to program effectiveness. Such information will be easier to obtain if outcome monitoring is already underway. Much of the data from the monitoring effort can likely be used directly in these studies. The procedures discussed here should also be useful for in-depth evaluation and analysis efforts in those studies where it is necessary to obtain special purpose information on client outcomes.

---

1. A related measurement approach, labeled Total Performance Measurement System (TPMS), has been formulated recently by the federal Joint Financial Management Improvement Program. As of this writing, it is being tested in a variety of agencies at the federal, state, and local level. It explicitly calls for client ratings, efficiency data, and employee attitude surveys. Measurement systems such as TPMS will also need effectiveness measurement information to provide a meaningful perspective on government performance.

Note that, by themselves, the outcome measurements discussed in this study do not generally indicate <u>why</u> a particular outcome occurred or <u>what</u> could be done to improve it.[1] Such a determination usually requires in-depth program evaluation or program analysis.

There has been a growing trend toward performance auditing, including program-results auditing, of government services and programs.[2] Such auditing may be sponsored by the legislative body or the chief executive. Program-results auditing is very similar to program evaluation; the principal distinction between them is probably the degree of independence of the auditors from the agency responsible for the programs. Such auditing depends heavily on adequate measurement of program effectiveness and quality. Similarly, the recent concern with "accountability" appears to require accountability for the outcomes of services as well as financial probity. Outcome measurements such as those discussed in this report would appear to be vital for such auditing and accountability purposes.

5. <u>Employee motivation</u>. The procedures described in this report are <u>not</u> intended to be used for assessing the performance of individual employees, such as caseworkers. Aggregate information on outcomes, however, can provide employees--especially managerial employees--with a "scorecard" on client outcomes as well as information on specific areas of agency performance, such as client ratings of the accessibility of social services. Such regular feedback to social service employees interested in the improvement of their clients may encourage them to seek ways to improve client outcomes.

The establishment of performance targets for social service agencies and managers could be undertaken more meaningfully with regularly collected, reliable outcome information. The development of performance targets in the public sector, including those undertaken as parts of Management by Objectives (MBO) efforts, has been greatly handicapped by lack of meaningful measures of the effectiveness and quality of services. Governments trying to focus on objective measures of performance have often been forced to rely primarily on measures of input, process, or workload. Unfortunately, reliance on such measures tends to encourage government employees to overemphasize certain aspects of their job, and this imbalance can cause deterioration of the overall quality of their work. Agencies attempting to use performance targets should find measures such as those discussed in this report useful for inclusion in their lists of objectives. They can help to ensure that service quality is explicitly addressed.

6. <u>Performance contracting</u>. Outcome data can be used in controlling and assessing the performance of outside contractors, whether the contractors are private agencies or other government agencies. The sample sizes suggested in this report would not, in general, be large enough to permit a state to

---

1. However, the client-satisfaction questions do ask clients about their perceptions of whether the help they received led to improvements (for example, see question 95 of Appendix A).

2. A major element in the initiation of this trend was the issuance in 1972 by the U.S. General Accounting Office of its <u>Standards for Audit of Governmental Organizations, Programs, Activities, and Functions</u> (Washington, D.C., 1972).

assess the client outcomes of individual contractors. If sample sizes were enlarged, however, the procedures could be used to make such assessments. Currently, few contracts include performance targets on outcomes, at least partly because the required data are rarely available on a regular basis. This application of the data would require careful consideration of the characteristics of incoming clients, especially client difficulty (discussed in Chapter 1), so that contractor performance could be assessed in relation to client mix.

7. Quality control checks on efficiency measurements. Governments which attempt to track the efficiency and productivity of their social services need to consider the quality as well as the quantity of work performed. Increases in work accomplished per dollar or per employee-hour (such as increases in "number of clients served per dollar") do not in themselves guarantee that real improvements in performance have occurred. Reductions in unit costs that occur at the expense of service quality should not be considered as efficiency or productivity improvements. Thus, a government should track the quality of services at the same time that it tracks unit costs. Outcome indicators such as those identified here are likely to be useful for such quality checks. At the very least, outcome data should be presented along with unit cost data so that public officials can obtain a perspective on how outcomes and unit costs are moving relative to each other.

8. Improved communication of citizens and clients with government officials. The systematic obtaining of feedback from representative samples of clients (including information on client satisfaction) and from representative samples of citizens is in itself a valuable feature of outcome measurement. Such feedback, if obtained and used properly, can be considered an important means of communication between citizens and social service agencies. With proper collection procedures, the information obtained will be considerably more representative of clients and citizens than information obtained from other common sources of citizen feedback, such as citizen complaints, personal observations by individual managers, or periodic contacts between officials and selected parts of the population. The survey approaches discussed in this report should provide considerably improved client and citizen feedback that government officials can use in making program and policy decisions.

In addition, the availability of outcome information can also enhance communication in the other direction, from government officials to citizens. Outcome indicators such as those discussed focus on service characteristics of direct concern to a jurisdiction's clients and its other citizens; citizens are likely to be less interested in level-of-activity (for example, workload) measures and other typical government statistics.

9. Local management control (a potential future use). If client follow-up procedures prove reliable and useful, the same basic procedures are also likely to be appropriate for use by individual county offices (whether state- or county-administered) in assessing the outcomes of their own clients. A modified form of the procedures might be developed for use with all clients rather than only a sample. This would help local offices with their own resource allocation and planning efforts.

Reporting Outcome Monitoring Data

    How the data are reported is likely to have an important impact on
whether and how the data are used. The information should be presented to
public officials in as concise, understandable, meaningful, and interesting
a fashion as possible. Unclear or overly long reports, especially ones
involving many statistics, should be avoided. The following suggestions may
help alleviate problems:

    1. Reports should emphasize comparisons that are of interest (rather than
merely presenting jurisdiction-wide totals), such as comparisons showing
changes or differences (a) from one year to the next; (b) among different
areas of the state; (c) in findings for different client groups; (d) for
various major modes of service delivery; and (e) between targeted performance
and actual performance.

    Exhibits 2 and 7 through 10 illustrate formats that might be used to
summarize findings. These formats are designed for upper-level management.
Findings on specific questions (such as those contained in Appendix A) and
specific indicators (such as those listed in Exhibit 1) could also be provided to upper-level management but are more likely to be of concern to
middle-level managers. The formats in Exhibits 2 and 7 through 10 can be
varied to make them useful to officials at various levels. Information on
the outcomes of specific programs, or in specific counties, can be provided
if the sample sizes for each are sufficiently large. (The exhibits express
outcomes in terms of "percentage of clients improved"; such percentages can
be obtained only if similar data are obtained on the same clients at both
intake and follow-up.)

    For information on unmet needs obtained from a statewide citizen survey,
formats such as those shown in Exhibits 5 and 6 (in Chapter 5) seem appropriate for summarizing the data concisely. (Putting the findings of a number of demographic categories on the same table, as shown in Exhibit 6,
relieves users of the need to review numerous pages of tables and permits
users to identify readily those demographic groups that appear to have
problems meriting attention.[1])

    After a citizen or client survey has been repeated annually over a period
of years, comparisons of major results over time should be undertaken. An
illustrative summary format which facilitates comparison of the current
year's client outcomes with those of previous years is shown in Exhibit 8.

_____

    1. Typically, survey results are presented on many individual sheets,
each of which provides one question tallied for one demographic category.
The format shown in Exhibit 6 can be generated manually by having clerical
personnel transfer information from individual computer sheets to the
illustrated format. An alternative is to use a computer program to generate
the form directly from the data. The Urban Institute has developed a computer
program for this purpose. Documentation on the program as well as a tape
copy can be obtained from The Urban Institute Computer Services Division:
J. Gueron and B. Ouyang, "UI-MCTAB: A Multiple Crosstab Program"
(Washington, D.C.: The Urban Institute, August 8, 1974).

2. It is highly desirable to have staff personnel review findings and summarize the highlights (that is, provide an "executive summary") for upper-level management and perhaps for the legislature. Oral summaries of the major findings are also likely to be desirable for some officials (who may be better reached in person than in writing).

3. The principle of "management by exception" also seems a good strategy for handling outcome data in reports to upper-level managers. To define systematically what constitutes an "exception," the government might select certain acceptable limits for (a) the magnitude of each indicator, (b) the magnitude of differences between population groups, and (c) the degree of change in the various indicators from one time period to the next. For example, the findings for each client group might be compared to the jurisdiction's overall results. Differences exceeding, say, ten percentage points might be highlighted.[1] Similarly, after data have been collected for more than one year, the government might determine acceptable limits for differences from the previous year's results. Any measure found to exceed these limits in the current year would be reported to upper-level management. Highlighting such "out of control" conditions might also be done by circling those findings on the reports.

4. It may be desirable to attempt to develop target values for the various outcome indicators after enough experience has been accumulated to permit realistic assessments of what is possible. Actual performance would subsequently be compared to the targets.[2] Exhibit 9 illustrates such a format.

The determination of targets can be difficult and complex, since there has been little experience with such measures. There are no national standards or comparative data on most of these measures. Our suggestion is that a government defer any substantive use of targets until a few years of experience are gained or until sufficient analysis of its social services has been undertaken so that the government can have some confidence that the targets are reasonable.

5. The reporting of outcome measurements should include feedback from program offices as to their views on the meaning of the findings and what might be done in response to them. Exhibit 11 presents an illustrative memo to program offices transmitting detailed findings and requesting reactions. The memo also suggests that these offices discuss the findings

---

1. For findings derived from samples, statistical "significance" should be considered; deviations likely to have resulted from the "luck-of-the-draw" should be so identified. It is not recommended, however, that statistical significance be used as the principal criterion for selecting areas of concern. With relatively large samples even a difference of, for example, three percentage points might be statistically significant, but such differences may be of little concern for program and policy decisions. It is recommended that "practical" significance be the primary criterion, with statistical significance used to supplement this information by identifying the likelihood that differences or changes were caused "by chance."

2. This approach has been used by some local governments such as New York; the District of Columbia; Charlotte, North Carolina; Fairfax County, Virginia; and Savannah, Georgia, though not, to our knowledge, in social services.

with their employees. In this way, outcome measurement findings can be used to provide feedback to government employees on the apparent results of their work and how their performance is perceived by clients.

Analyzing Outcome Monitoring Data

The previous sections have suggested some basic analyses of outcome data, such as comparing current findings against previous years, comparisons of outcomes from various client groups, and comparisons of actual outcomes against targeted outcomes. The presentation of such data will provide government officials with information on problems, progress, and trends in social services. The data can also be subjected to more extensive analysis. Suggestions for additional analysis follow.

1. There are a number of straightforward types of analyses that require relatively small amounts of analytical time. These include calculations of the percentage of change from one time period to another and, after more than two years of data are available, analysis of the time series to indicate long-term trends. Time-trend lines can also be used to provide a baseline against which actual future values, occurring after major program changes have been made, can be compared, thus giving a rough indication of the effect of those program changes.

2. A variety of additional cross-tabulations can be made to provide further insights as to what has happened. For example, progress on various dimensions can be related to information on the type and length of services provided to clients to indicate the apparent relation of these to various client outcomes.

3. Analysis of the distribution of clients at intake as to levels of difficulty and each level's outcome may provide added insights in terms of the type of clients being served (or not being served) and suggest possible changes in program emphasis.

4. Numerous factors unamenable to government and agency control can affect outcomes. For example, major changes in national and state economic conditions during the year can significantly affect outcomes on self-support. Because of such possibilities, it would be desirable to have staff personnel identify important external events that may help to explain observed changes in outcomes. This opens the door to "excuses," but if such explanations are examined objectively the added information should be worthwhile. Government analysts should keep track of such factors and consider them when summarizing performance results. Operating agencies, of course, can be of considerable assistance in the identification of external factors that affect their performance.

Analyses might also be undertaken to consider the relation of outcomes in various geographical areas to characteristics that may explain differences

among regions. Unemployment rates or poor public transportation, for
example, may be found to be highly correlated with differences in outcomes
among areas. These analyses could then help to provide a basis for the
determination of different outcome targets in various areas. For example,
areas with higher unemployment rates might be expected to show fewer improvements in employment status than others.

Conclusion: The Value of Adequate Resources and Time

To get the most value from outcome information, a government will need
to apply adequate resources to analytical efforts. Governments undertaking
an outcome-monitoring program are likely to find that additional payoffs occur
even if only a small level of analysis is provided. Such analysis should
examine not only the outcome information but also other relevant information,
including data on costs, program characteristics, and external factors (as
noted above). Lack of analytical resources in governments has been, and
will continue to be, a major constraint on the use of performance data,
whether effectiveness or efficiency data.

The types of data discussed in this study can provide significantly
improved information about government programs and policies, but without
a determined effort to apply resources to data analysis and to utilize the
results, the effort spent for its collection can be wasted. If a government does not think it will use outcome information, or if it undertakes
such measurement and subsequently finds that it is not using the information,
the measurement effort should be discontinued, but only after sufficient
trial. Efforts during the first year or two can be discouraging, at least
until public managers and other officials have sufficient opportunity to
consider the information's various uses and gain some confidence in its
meaningfulness and reliability.

EXHIBIT 7

ILLUSTRATIVE FORMAT FOR SOCIAL SERVICES CLIENT OUTCOME FINDINGS: BY GOAL BY REGION[a]

1978

Goal[b]	Total State[c]				Region I				Region II				Region III			
	Number of Clients	% Improved	% Same	% Worsened	Number of Clients	% Improved	% Same	% Worsened	Number of Clients	% Improved	% Same	% Worsened	Number of Clients	% Improved	% Same	% Worsened
1																
2																
3																
4																
5																
Total																

a. Various types of geographical subdivisions could be used here. North Carolina, for example, has four administrative regions for social services. Groups of counties are another possibility.

b. Refers to the five goals of Title XX. States may want to base this on the "primary goal" of each client. Most clients have multiple goals, however, since they often have multiple problems.

c. "Improved" and "worsened" need to be defined specifically in a systematic way, based on responses to the questionnaire.

EXHIBIT 8

ILLUSTRATIVE FORMAT FOR SOCIAL SERVICES CLIENT OUTCOME FINDINGS:
CLIENT CONDITION OR CATEGORY BY YEAR[a]

Region I

Client Condition or Category at Entry[b]	1977				1978				1979			
	Number of Clients	% Improved[c]	% Same	% Worsened	Number of Clients	% Improved	% Same	% Worsened	Number of Clients	% Improved	% Same	% Worsened
Category 1												
Category 2												
Category 3												
Category 4												
Category 5												
Total												

a. This table can be used to show trends over time either for the state as a whole or for particular regions.

b. These could be "severity of problem" categories or demographic characteristic categories, for example, various age groups, types of problems, etc. Each such type of categorization could, by itself, be the subject of a separate table.

c. "Improved" and "worsened" need to be defined specifically in a systematic way, based on responses to the questionnaire.

EXHIBIT 9

ILLUSTRATIVE FORMAT FOR SOCIAL SERVICES CLIENT OUTCOME FINDINGS:
ACTUAL VERSUS PLANNED[a] PERCENTAGE OF CLIENTS IMPROVED[b]

1978

Client Condition or Category at Entry[c]	Total State		Region I		Region II		Region III		Region IV	
	% Planned	% Actual	% Planned	% Actual	% Planned	% Actual	% Planned	% Actual	% Planned	% Actual
Category 1										
Category 2										
Category 3										
Category 4										
Category 5										
Total										

a. The "planned" estimates probably should be derived after obtaining one or two years' initial data from the outcome-monitoring procedures. The estimates could be based on experiences in prior years, and on program analyses of likely outcomes from the scheduled resource allocations.

b. "Improvement" must be defined specifically in terms of the items in the data collection instrument.

c. These could be "severity of problem" categories or demographic characteristic categories, for example, various age groups or types of problems. Each such type of categorization could, by itself, be the subject of a separate table.

EXHIBIT 10

ILLUSTRATIVE FORMAT FOR SOCIAL SERVICES OUTCOME MONITORING:
CLIENT CONDITION AT ENTRY AND AT FOLLOW-UP[c]

Region I[a]

Client Condition at Entry[b] \ Client Condition at Follow-Up	Category 1	Category 2	Category 3	Category 4	Category 5
Category 1					
Category 2					
Category 3					
Category 4					
Category 5					
Total					

a. Such tables would need to be drawn up for each region or major geographical subdivision.

b. These could be "severity" of problem conditions or "difficulty" categories that indicate client status at a given time.

c. The data presented could be the percentage of those in each entry condition that were in each category at the time of follow-up.

EXHIBIT 11

ILLUSTRATIVE MEMO TO OPERATING OFFICES TRANSMITTING DETAILED
CLIENT FOLLOW-UP FINDINGS AND REQUESTING AGENCY VIEWS

To: Operating Offices

From: Department/Division Head

Subject: Results of 1976 Client Follow-up Effort

Attached are the results of the client follow-up effort conducted in 1976.
During the survey, 2,500 clients were interviewed. The survey procedures were
based on modern survey techniques. Hence, although they were based on only a
small percentage of the total number of clients, they provide a more representative cross section of client views than can be obtained by most other means,
such as casual contacts or complaint data. These findings on clients can
therefore be considered to be approximately representative of the state's
social service clients.

Client outcomes after receiving services are a vital concern to us all.
I would like to have your office's views as to what you believe are the highlights and implications of these findings for government programs and policies.
Please review these findings carefully, looking particularly at differences in
response by geographical area, age group, type of client problem, race, and sex.

In your reply, please address the following questions:

1. What are the significant findings, for example, the apparent problem
    areas, particular groups or areas needing attention--and the major
    successes?

2. What might explain the reasons for these problem areas or apparent
    successes? (This is not likely to be apparent from these findings;
    you will need to draw on your own insights and other agency infor-
    mation.)

3. What actions should be considered to alleviate the problems or to
    expand on the successes?

In addition to providing information that may be of assistance to you in
planning your program this year, it is hoped that these findings will become
a baseline for comparisons with similar future surveys that we plan to undertake on an annual basis.

You may want to take the opportunity to discuss the findings of the survey
with employees in your organization, both to obtain their suggestions and to
provide them with a clearer perspective as to client outcomes and perceptions
of the services they are providing.

I would like to provide the governor and the legislature with a summary
report in approximately five weeks. This will be based in part on the material
provided by you. Please provide the results of your review to my office in
three weeks. Subsequent discussions, if needed, will be held to clarify the
findings and to discuss any subsequent actions that seem appropriate.

Chapter 7

IMPLEMENTATION ISSUES

This chapter is devoted to issues in the implementation of social service outcome-monitoring procedures by a state.[1]

Assigning Responsibility for Outcome-Monitoring

One of the first issues is determining which agency is to be responsible for the monitoring. The social service agency may be a part of a larger department, as in the case of North Carolina's Department of Human Resources and Wisconsin's Department of Health and Social Services, or it may be a department by itself. The group responsible for social service outcome monitoring should probably be an evaluation unit in the department, or in the social service division. Another, but less likely, possibility would be to assign the responsibility to a central staff office of the government. Regardless of which agency is primarily responsible, it is crucial that personnel from the social services division have a major role in planning and carrying out the monitoring. Active participation by social service personnel from the beginning is likely to be an essential part of the success of any evaluation effort.

In North Carolina a task force consisting of employees from the evaluation unit of the Department of Human Resources, personnel from the Division of Social Services, and members of the Budget and Planning Offices of the Department of Administration were given responsibility for the development and implementation of the monitoring effort. The task force was chaired by a member of the planning section of the Division of Social Services.

One of the first tasks for such a task force is to obtain the support of upper-level management, both in the division and in the department. Such support should include periodic encouragement of the monitoring team, consistent backing in the face of the occasional but inevitable obstacles that arise, and provision of adequate staff and financial resources. Moreover, there are some choices affecting methodology that require management input (such as choice of categories of clients for which management seeks outcome information).

---

1. This discussion draws extensively from the North Carolina-Urban Institute experiences during 1975-76. North Carolina pretested the questionnaire in Appendix A but has not yet undertaken either a pilot test of the entire procedure or full implementation.

The task force will probably do much work in developing and implementing the procedures, but this work will often be in the form of coordinating the efforts of a variety of other persons. Activities that will have to be coordinated (or developed by the task force) for both the client outcome monitoring and unmet needs assessment procedures include:

(1) Identification of the specific outcomes to be monitored, including the various dimensions and indicators of performance (see, for example, Chapters 1 and 5 and Exhibit 1),

(2) Development of the instruments for collecting the information (see Chapters 1 and 5 and Appendices A and B),

(3) Selection of the procedures for sampling clients (including the various issues discussed in Chapter 3),

(4) Pretests of the data collection instruments,

(5) Pilot tests of the "full procedures," perhaps in two or three counties,

(6) Selection of the procedures for scoring the findings (see Chapter 2), and

(7) Development of data displays that will be most useful to public officials (see Chapter 6).

In North Carolina the task force selected an initial set of outcomes of social services in terms of the dimensions relating to the five goals of Title XX. For each dimension the task force identified specific items of information believed necessary to formulate questions.[1] This is a critical step so that state personnel can identify the outcome information relevant to social services from which a questionnaire can be developed.

The initial set of outcomes should be thoroughly reviewed by others in the agency. For example, state regional offices and county offices should also be given the opportunity to participate in the development of the procedures, at a minimum through review of project materials.

In addition, the task force should examine any computerized procedures available for collecting data within the agency. An existing data system may provide a framework from which to draw the sample of clients and in some cases may provide demographic information on clients in the sample.

Cooperation with County-Level and Private Delivery Organizations

Another significant issue is that of state-county and state-private agency relations in developing and implementing outcome-monitoring procedures. This

---

1. The choice of items was sometimes limited by whether they seemed measurable and whether specific questions could be formulated that appeared to have at least some face validity.

applies particularly to states where social services are state-supervised
but county-administered; eighteen states have such social service systems;
the rest are state-administered.[1] Whether state- or county-administered,
it is important that county office cooperation and participation be obtained
as early as possible. The evaluation team should maintain close communication with county social service directors about the purpose and development
of the monitoring effort. It is highly desirable to involve these offices
(or their specified representatives) in the development of the procedures.[2]

An advisory group consisting of representatives of both regional and
local offices as well as selected nongovernment social service organizations
seems highly desirable.

In North Carolina the state created an advisory committee consisting of
various county directors, regional officials, representatives of private
agencies (such as United Way), professional organizations, and clients. This
committee reviewed the questionnaire and other procedures.[3] As a result,
the state task force made alterations based on the advisory committee's
review. Such a review should, of course, be taken seriously and should not be
hurried. The advisory committee can be quite helpful in getting local offices
and other service delivery agencies to cooperate with, implement, and use
outcome monitoring.

The state should attempt to identify for county representatives what
they can hope to gain from monitoring outcomes. County directors and casework supervisors are more likely to be helpful if they can see the value to
themselves of such an effort. The evaluation team should identify the kind
of information that will result, and why it would be useful to these other
officials. Private agencies that are state-funded or have contracts with
county social service agencies should be similarly advised.

In North Carolina (this can also be expected elsewhere), county officials
expressed considerable anxiety about the possibility that the state would
"misuse" the information obtained from monitoring. Advisory committee members

---

1. J. Turem et al., "Planning for Social Services: The Title XX Experience,"
Working Paper 0990-01 (Washington, D.C.: The Urban Institute, October 1975)
p. 141.

2. One suggestion made by a member of the North Carolina Advisory Committee
was that states should provide the conceptual and technological assistance
and let counties conduct their own monitoring. The member felt that states
should be concerned with the mechanics of administering Title XX rather than
the outcomes on clients. Although this position may be extreme, it highlights
the need for close state-county cooperation.

3. The North Carolina task force found that for the questionnaire to make
sense to reviewers, the latter should be provided with a statement of purpose
of its intended use, the rationale for the various items included (such as
that provided in Chapter 1), and their relationship to the indicators of
client status and the goals of Title XX.

pointed out that, given the methodological weakness in evaluations of social service programs, the data obtained would have to be interpreted cautiously. One remarked, "I'm afraid they will try to make the wrong kinds of decisions on the data. For example, I can just see the State Social Services Commission deciding to cut out half of the projects because one of the tables that you produced says that these programs show only 10 percent improvement in clients."

Any form of evaluation tends to induce such anxiety, and two steps can be taken to alleviate it:

(1) Spell out the caveats and gaps in knowledge. It is important, for example, that managers, legislators, budgeters, and the public not confuse outcome-monitoring results with causal inferences derived from in-depth program analysis or from rigorous experimental techniques.[1] Outcome monitoring is limited in what it can achieve, and it is crucial that decision makers and evaluators understand its limitations. Nonetheless, it can, when used properly, provide useful information which states often lack now.

(2) The state should try to make it clear who are the potential users of the data (for example, state management, county directors, legislators), and how it is to be used. Potential uses, such as those discussed in Chapter 6, should be discussed with management personnel, perhaps using the output formats as illustrations. The task force should guard against possible misuse of these data by management personnel. It may be help-ful for the team to identify both the ways in which each type of potential user might use the outcome data and the ways in which the data should not be used because of technical limitations.

Counties are understandably anxious about an evaluation conducted at the state level that may lead to changes in resource allocation. County participation is another method of reducing such anxiety. Similarly useful would be assurances that the state will not make resource allocations based solely or even primarily on outcome-monitoring findings--at least not until sufficient experience with the data has been gained and its reliability in-dicated. It is also highly desirable to give individual county offices the opportunity to review and comment on outcome findings before resource alloca-tion decisions are made. For example, local offices might be asked to indicate reasons for apparently "poor" or "good" performance.[2]

---

1. Users of the information should be made aware of the lack of causality and, as far as possible, the extent of measurement error and bias in the information provided. Users of the data must be educated about the limitations of the information as well as its uses.

2. Exhibit 11 in Chapter 6 shows how such a review might be requested.

Caseworkers are also likely to be anxious about the possible use of outcome-monitoring data by supervisors, county directors, or state central offices to evaluate individual performance. Monitoring is not intended for such a purpose, and the evaluation team should clarify that point with the advisory group and with other persons in the field.

Nevertheless, outcome information may be useful to individual case-workers. This depends on whether the county sample size is large enough to allow caseworkers to see the outcomes of their collective efforts. Caseworkers, in any case, will be interested in a questionnaire that is to be administered to their clients and ex-clients.

In North Carolina caseworker supervisors were afraid that monitoring would result in extra work for them.[1] This need not be the case, if, as we have recommended, caseworkers are not asked to undertake the follow-up survey of clients. The state team should make both county and state responsibilities clear to those in the field.

Maintenance of Confidentiality

Clients' individual responses must be kept confidential. Records of interviews conducted for monitoring should not be placed in their case records, and such information should be accessible only to interviewers and analysts. Users should obtain outcome data only in aggregate form. Safeguards must be provided. The voluntary nature of participation, and a guarantee of confidentiality, should be made clear to each client (and to interviewers) before a consent form is signed by the client, and before those in the follow-up samples are interviewed.

A Final Word

There are major technical problems in developing a meaningful and reliable social service outcome-monitoring process. The resolution of these problems will require considerable effort and care. Much of the desired success of this effort will depend on the ability of the implementing task force to deal with the politics of the implementation process--to keep in close touch with the many interested parties, to explain the details, and to get various persons interested and involved. The temptation to rush ahead with the technical steps while ignoring the interests of the various organizations concerned will be great. This temptation must be strongly resisted if the goal is to obtain both a better product and one which is broadly accepted and used.

---

1. Local offices and caseworkers, often for good reason, tend to be irritated when states impose frequent changes in information requirements.

Appendix A

ILLUSTRATIVE SET OF QUESTIONS FOR MONITORING CLIENT OUTCOMES*

BACKGROUND INFORMATION

A. Client #_____

B. Racial or ethnic group _____

C. Age _____years

D. Sex _____Male _____Female

E. Address _____

F. Type of residence:

_____Private home
_____"Home" for the aged (including senior citizen hotels, group homes, old age homes)
_____Prison
_____Juvenile correction facility
_____General hospital
_____State psychiatric hospital
_____State center for the retarded
_____Jail
_____Specialty hospital
_____School for the blind
_____School for the deaf
_____Skilled nursing facility
_____Intermediate nursing facility

G. Telephone no. _____
                   Area code   Number   Extension

H. Marital status _____Single   _____Married   _____Separated
                    _____Divorced   _____Widowed

I. Other members of household:

Relationship to Respondent	Age	Sex		Relationship to Respondent	Age	Sex
a._____	____	____		e._____	____	____
b._____	____	____		f._____	____	____
c._____	____	____		g._____	____	____
d._____	____	____		h._____	____	____

_____

*This is not intended to be a questionnaire that is ready for administration to clients; hence detailed instructions have not been provided for interviewers, nor has the order of the questions been considered in terms of what order is most likely to yield maximum respondent cooperation. Not all sections are to be administered to each client. For example, sections II and III would probably not need to be asked in an in-person interview of a clearly able-bodied person. (See Chapter 2 for a preliminary exploration of which sections are appropriate for which client groups.) The questions contained here are worded for in-person interviews; revisions will be needed for telephone interviews.

J. Level of education:

     _____B.A. or higher
     _____Some college
     _____High school graduate
     _____Completed 9th grade
     _____Completed 6th grade
     _____Less than 6 years of schooling

K. Types of jobs held in past year (level of job experience):*

a._____

b._____

c._____

d._____

L. Disability or impairment, if any:

M. Types of problems the client has had in the previous year:

a._____

b._____

c._____

d._____

N. Types of services and length of time each service was provided during the previous year:

Service Provided	Beginning Date	Termination Date
a.		
b.		
c.		
d.		

---

*To be coded at the time of analysis.

QUESTIONS FOR ASSESSING CLIENT OUTCOMES

I. Economic Self-Support

1. What is your main activity now? (MULTIPLE RESPONSES PERMITTED)

    _____Employed full-time
    _____Employed part-time
    _____Attending school or a training program
    _____Unemployed or not attending school or training program
    _____(IF SO) Why is that? _____
    _____Unable to work
    _____(IF SO) Why is that? _____
    _____Keeping house for self
    _____Retired
    _____Volunteer work (no pay or "pay only for expenses")
    _____Other (specify) _____

2. Approximately how many months/weeks of the past three months were you employed?

    _____Months/weeks

3. In the past three months, during the time you were working, what kinds of jobs did you have? (LIST ALL JOBS HELD FOR AT LEAST ONE WEEK)

    a._____
    b._____
    c._____
    d._____

4. For each job you mentioned above, (a) how long did you work at the job, (b) was it part-time or full-time, and (c) how much did you get paid?

Job	Length of Time	Full-time or Part-time	If Part-time, How Many Hours Per Week	Pay (Per Hour, Week, Month or Year)
a._____	_____	_____	_____	_____
b._____	_____	_____	_____	_____
c._____	_____	_____	_____	_____
d._____	_____	_____	_____	_____

5. During the past three months, did you or any other member of your family receive any money from the following? About how much?

                                                                Who received it?

    $_____Unemployment compensation or workmen's compensation   _____
    $_____Welfare payments, aid to dependent children   _____
    $_____Food stamps   _____
    $_____Salaries, pensions, and other private support   _____
    $_____Other (specify) _____   _____

II. Ability to Undertake Activities of Daily Living

6. In the past month, did someone help you feed yourself?

_____ Yes (ASK a, b, AND d)
_____ No   (ASK c AND d)

a. How did this person help you? (for example, cut food, spread butter, open cartons)

_____
_____
_____

b. If you didn't have someone to help you, would you have been able to (REPEAT EACH RESPONSE GIVEN IN a)

_____ Yes _____ No _____ Don't know
_____ Yes _____ No _____ Don't know
_____ Yes _____ No _____ Don't know

c. Do you feel you needed help? (for example, to cut food, spread butter, open cartons)

_____ Yes (please explain) _____
_____ No

d. Have you needed any special devices, such as utensils with enlarged handles, forked knife, and so forth, to help you feed yourself?

_____ Yes (please explain) _____
_____ No

7. In the past month, did someone help you dress and undress yourself?

_____ Yes (ASK a, b, AND d)
_____ No   (ASK c AND d)

a. How did this person help you? (for example, fasten hooks, buttons or zippers; get clothing from closet or drawer)

_____
_____
_____

b. If you didn't have someone to help you, would you have been able to (REPEAT EACH RESPONSE GIVEN IN a)

_____ Yes _____ No _____ Don't know
_____ Yes _____ No _____ Don't know
_____ Yes _____ No _____ Don't know

c. Do you feel you needed help? (for example, to fasten hooks, buttons, or zippers; get clothing from closet or drawer; tie shoelaces; get shoes on correct feet)

_____ Yes (please explain) _____
_____ No

d. Have you needed any special devices, such as long-handled shoe horns, zipper pulls, and so forth, to help dress yourself?

_____ Yes (please explain) _____
_____ No

8. In the past month, did someone help you take a bath or shower?

_____ Yes (ASK a, b, AND d)
_____ No   (ASK c AND d)

a. How did this person help you? (for example, get the water ready, get towel and soap, bathe yourself, get in and out of tub)

_____
_____
_____

b. If you didn't have someone to help you, would you have been able to (REPEAT EACH RESPONSE GIVEN IN a)

_____ Yes _____ No _____ Don't know
_____ Yes _____ No _____ Don't know
_____ Yes _____ No _____ Don't know

c. Do you feel that you needed help? (for example, to get the water ready, get the towel and soap, bathe yourself, or get in and out of the tub)

_____Yes (please explain) _____
_____No

d. Have you needed any special devices, such as handrails, pedal- or knee-controlled faucet, and so forth?

_____Yes (please explain) _____
_____No

9. In the past month, did someone help you use the bathroom?

_____Yes (ASK a, b, AND d)
_____No (ASK c AND d)

a. How did this person help you? (for example, get to and from the bathroom, transfer on and off the toilet seat, cleanse yourself)

b. If you didn't have someone to help you, would you have been able to (REPEAT EACH RESPONSE GIVEN IN a)

_____   _____Yes _____No _____Don't know
_____   _____Yes _____No _____Don't know
_____   _____Yes _____No _____Don't know

c. Do you feel that you needed help? (for example, to get to and from the bathroom, transfer on and off the toilet seat, cleanse yourself)

_____Yes (please explain)_____
_____No

d. Have you needed any special devices, like raised toilet seats, handrails, and so forth, to help you use the bathroom?

_____Yes (please explain) _____
_____No

10. In the past month, did someone help you take care of your appearance, like comb your hair, shave (for men), and so forth?

_____Yes (ASK a AND b)
_____No (ASK c)

a. How did this person help you? (for example, wash your hair, comb your hair, shave (for men), cut your fingernails and toenails, brush your teeth)

b. If you didn't have someone to help you, would you have been able to (REPEAT EACH RESPONSE GIVEN IN a)

_____   _____Yes _____No _____Don't know
_____   _____Yes _____No _____Don't know
_____   _____Yes _____No _____Don't know

c. Do you feel that you needed help? (for example, to wash your hair, comb your hair, shave (for men), cut your fingernails and toenails, brush your teeth)

_____Yes (please explain) _____
_____No

11. I'd like to ask you about how much you can move outside as well as inside the house. Can you (READ RESPONSES: STOP AFTER THE FIRST "YES")

_____Walk a mile or more without help of any kind?
_____Walk a mile or more without any help but with some difficulty?
_____Walk or transport yourself for a mile or more with adaptive devices (such as wheelchair, cane or walker)?
_____Walk or transport yourself for a mile or more but only with someone else along?
_____Move around the house with help from another person (this includes using wheelchair, cane, and so forth)?
_____Sit alone and propel wheelchair around the house but need help getting into and out of the wheelchair?
_____Do you need to have the wheelchair pushed by someone?
_____Are you bedfast?

III. Ability to Undertake "Instrumental" Activities of Daily Living

12. In the past month, did someone help you prepare meals?

    _____ Yes   (ASK a AND b)
    _____ No   (ASK c)

    a. How did this person help you?   b. If you didn't have someone to help you,
       (for example, plan meals so you get   would you have been able to (REPEAT EACH
       an adequate diet, prepare ingredients,   RESPONSE GIVEN IN a)
       make the entire meal and serve it to
       you)

       _____   _____ Yes   _____ No   _____ Don't know
       _____   _____ Yes   _____ No   _____ Don't know
                                                   _____ Yes   _____ No   _____ Don't know

    c. Do you feel you needed help? (for example, to plan meals so you get an adequate diet,
       prepare ingredients, make the entire meal, and serve it)

       _____ Yes (please explain) _____
       _____ No

13. In the past month, did someone help you with housework?

    _____ Yes   (ASK a AND b)
    _____ No   (ASK c)

    a. How did this person help you?   b. If you didn't have someone to help you,
       (for example, do light housework like   would you have been able to (REPEAT EACH
       dusting, dishwashing, bedmaking; do   RESPONSE GIVEN IN a)
       heavy work like cleaning floors)

       _____   _____ Yes   _____ No   _____ Don't know
       _____   _____ Yes   _____ No   _____ Don't know
                                                   _____ Yes   _____ No   _____ Don't know

    c. Do you feel that you needed help? (for example, with light housework like dusting, dish-
       washing, bedmaking; heavy work like cleaning floors)

       _____ Yes (please explain) _____
       _____ No

14. In the past month, did someone help you use the telephone?

    _____ Yes   (ASK a AND b)
    _____ No   (ASK c)

    a. How did this person help you?   b. If you didn't have someone to help you,
       (for example, look up numbers so   would you have been able to (REPEAT EACH
       you could dial, dial the telephone,   RESPONSE GIVEN IN a)
       write down messages)

       _____   _____ Yes   _____ No   _____ Don't know
       _____   _____ Yes   _____ No   _____ Don't know
                                                   _____ Yes   _____ No   _____ Don't know

    c. Do you feel that you needed help? (for example, to look up numbers, dial the telephone,
       take messages)

       _____ Yes (please explain) _____
       _____ No

15. In the past month, did someone help you go shopping for routine things like groceries or clothes (assuming you had transportation)?

_____Yes (ASK *a* AND *b*)
_____No   (ASK *c*)

a. How did this person help you?
   (for example, give and make change,
   go with you only when there are heavy
   packages to be carried, go with you
   on all shopping trips)

   _____
   _____
   _____

b. If you didn't have someone to help you,
   would you have been able to (REPEAT EACH
   RESPONSE GIVEN IN *a*)

   _____Yes _____No _____Don't know
   _____Yes _____No _____Don't know
   _____Yes _____No _____Don't know

c. Do you feel that you needed help? (for example, to give and make change, carry heavy packages, go with you on all shopping trips)

   _____Yes (please explain) _____
   _____No

16. In the past month, did someone help you do your laundry (assuming that you were able to get to the laundry)?

_____Yes (ASK *a* AND *b*)
_____No   (ASK *c*)

a. How did this person help you?
   (for example, separate clothes, measure
   soap, carry clothes to the laundry
   machine and back)

   _____
   _____
   _____

b. If you didn't have someone to help you,
   would you have been able to (REPEAT EACH
   RESPONSE GIVEN IN *a*)

   _____Yes _____No _____Don't know
   _____Yes _____No _____Don't know
   _____Yes _____No _____Don't know

c. Do you feel that you needed help? (for example, to separate clothes, measure soap, carry clothes to the laundry machine and back)

   _____Yes (please explain) _____
   _____No

17. In the past month, did someone help you take your medicine, if you take any?

_____Yes (ASK *a* AND *b*)
_____No   (ASK *c*)
_____Not applicable (didn't take medicine)   (GO TO NEXT QUESTION)

a. How did this person help you?
   (for example, remind you to take
   medicine at the right times, open
   bottles, give you the right dosage)

   _____
   _____
   _____

b. If you didn't have someone to help you,
   would you have been able to (REPEAT EACH
   RESPONSE GIVEN IN *a*)

   _____Yes _____No _____Don't know
   _____Yes _____No _____Don't know
   _____Yes _____No _____Don't know

c. Do you feel you needed help? (for example, to remember to take medicine at the right times, open bottles, get the right dosage)

   _____Yes (please explain) _____
   _____No

18. In the past month, have you been able to get to places beyond walking distance (READ RESPONSES)

_____Without help (drive a car, or use public/private transportation like buses, and so forth)?
_____With the help of special devices (for example, a specially made car)?
_____With some help (for example, must be shown which buses to take, assisted with straps)?
_____With considerable help (for example, take taxis only, or need someone to go with you when traveling)?
_____Are you unable to travel without special vehicles for the handicapped, ambulance, or some other special arrangement?

IV. Physical Health

19. During the past three months, how many days were you so sick that you were unable to carry on your usual activities--such as going to work or working around the house?

_____None
_____A week or less
_____More than a week but less than one month
_____A month or more but less than two months
_____Two months or more
_____Don't know

20. Did you go to the hospital anytime <u>as an in-patient</u> in the past three months?

_____Yes   (ASK *a*)
_____No   (GO TO NEXT QUESTION)

a. For how many days?   _____days (approximately)

21. How would you rate your overall health in the past three months? (READ RESPONSES)

_____Good
_____Fair
_____Poor
_____Don't know

22. In the past three months, how much have your health troubles stood in the way of your doing the things you wanted to do? (READ RESPONSES)

_____Not at all
_____A little (some)
_____A great deal
_____Don't know

23. (FOR FOLLOW-UP ONLY)
When you compare your health now to what it was like before you started receiving help from (name of agency), would you say it is <u>now</u> (READ RESPONSES)

_____Much better
_____Somewhat better
_____About the same
_____Somewhat worse
_____Don't know

V. Mental Distress

24. In the past month, how often have you felt <u>fearful</u> or <u>afraid</u>? (READ RESPONSES)

_____Never
_____Once or twice
_____Often
_____Almost always

25. In the past month, how often have you felt <u>sad</u> or <u>depressed</u>? (READ RESPONSES)

_____Never
_____Once or twice
_____Often
_____Almost always

26. In the past month, how often have you felt <u>angry</u>? (READ RESPONSES)

_____Never
_____Once or twice
_____Often
_____Almost always

27. In the past month, how often have you felt <u>mixed up</u> or <u>confused</u>? (READ RESPONSES)

_____Never
_____Once or twice
_____Often
_____Almost always

28. In the past month, how often have you felt <u>tense</u> or <u>uptight</u>? (READ RESPONSES)

_____Never
_____Once or twice
_____Often
_____Almost always

29. In the past month, have you had trouble <u>sleeping</u>? (READ RESPONSES)

_____Never
_____Once or twice
_____Often
_____Almost always

30. In the past month, have you had trouble with <u>headaches</u>? (READ RESPONSES)

_____Never
_____Once or twice
_____Often
_____Almost always

31. In the past month, have you had trouble with <u>poor appetite</u>? (READ RESPONSES)

_____Never
_____Once or twice
_____Often
_____Almost always

32. In the past month, have you had trouble with an <u>upset stomach</u>? (READ RESPONSES)

_____Never
_____Once or twice
_____Often
_____Almost always

33. In the past month, have you had trouble with <u>feeling very tired</u>? (READ RESPONSES)

_____Never
_____Once or twice
_____Often
_____Almost always

(CALCULATE SCORE FOR 24-33)

34. In the past month, how often have you felt you can't cope with things? (READ RESPONSES)

_____Never
_____Once or twice
_____Often
_____Almost always

35. In the past month, have you ever been so upset that someone had to come in and take care of you?

_____Yes   For how many days? _____
_____No
_____Don't know

36. In the past month, how often did you feel you did not want to go on living? (READ RESPONSES)

_____Never
_____Once or twice
_____Often
_____Almost always

37. In the past month, did you have as much contact as you would like with a person (or persons) that you felt close to--somebody that you could trust and confide in?

_____Yes
_____No
_____Don't know

38. In the past month, did you see your relatives and friends as often as you wanted to, or were you somewhat unhappy about how little you saw them, or were you considerably unhappy about how little you saw them?

_____As often as you wanted to
_____Somewhat unhappy about how little you saw them
_____Considerably unhappy about how little you saw them
_____Don't know

39. Over the past month, did you find yourself feeling quite lonely? (READ RESPONSES)

_____Almost never
_____Sometimes
_____Often
_____Almost always
_____Don't know

40. Taking everything into consideration, how would you describe your satisfaction with life in general at the present time? (READ RESPONSES)

_____Good
_____Fair
_____Not sure
_____Poor

41. (FOR FOLLOW-UP ONLY)
    Since you started getting help from (name of agency) are your problems (READ RESPONSES)

_____Much better
_____Somewhat better
_____About the same
_____Somewhat worse
_____Much worse

VI. Alcohol and Drug Abuse

42. In the past month, about how often did you drink alcohol? (READ RESPONSES)

_____Almost never (no drinking at all or less than one drink per week)
_____Occasionally (up to three drinks per week, but no more)
_____Often (four or more drinks per week)

(ASK QUESTIONS 43-45 ONLY IF RESPONSE TO QUESTION 42 IS "OCCASIONALLY" OR "OFTEN")

43. Has your drinking caused any difficulties or problems for you in your emotional or physical health in the past month? (READ RESPONSES)

_____Never
_____Sometimes
_____Often
_____Almost always
_____Don't know

44. Has your drinking caused any problems with your employer or job in the past month? (READ RESPONSES)

_____Never
_____Sometimes
_____Often
_____Almost always
_____Don't know

45. Has your drinking caused any difficulties or problems with your family or your friends in the past month? (READ RESPONSES)

_____Never
_____Sometimes
_____Often
_____Almost always
_____Don't know

46. In the past month, have you been arrested for public drunkenness or drinking-related charges?

_____Yes   How many times? _____
_____No
_____Don't know

47. Do you feel you have an alcohol problem?

_____Yes   (ASK a)
_____No   (GO TO NEXT QUESTION)
_____Don't know   (GO TO NEXT QUESTION)

a. Are you getting any help for the problem?

_____Getting help (Alcoholics Anonymous, private clinic, etc.)
_____Doesn't feel he/she needs help
_____Received help but feels it did no good
_____Seeking help
_____Not sure what to do about it

48. In the past month, did you use drugs of any kind other than alcohol?

_____Yes   (ASK *a*)
_____No   (GO TO NEXT QUESTION)

a. Which drugs did you use, and how often?

_____Heroin: _____ times per _____
_____Morphine: _____ times per _____
_____Cocaine: _____ times per _____
_____Amphetamines: _____ times per _____
_____Barbiturates: _____ times per _____
_____Other (specify) _____
_____
_____

(ASK QUESTIONS 49-51 ONLY IF RESPONSE TO QUESTION 48 IS "YES")

49. Has your use of drugs caused you any problems in your emotional or physical health in the past month?

_____Never
_____Sometimes
_____Often
_____All the time
_____Don't know

50. Has your use of drugs caused any problems with your employer or job in the past month?

_____Never
_____Sometimes
_____Often
_____All the time
_____Don't know

51. Has your use of drugs caused any problems with your family or friends in the past month?

_____Never
_____Sometimes
_____Often
_____All the time
_____Don't know

52. In the past month, have you been arrested for illegal possession or use of drugs?

_____Yes   How many times? _____
_____No
_____Don't know

53. Do you feel you have a drug problem?

_____Yes   (ASK *a*)
_____No   (GO TO NEXT QUESTION)
_____Don't know   (GO TO NEXT QUESTION)

a. Are you getting any help for the problem?

_____Getting help (Synanon, methadone treatment, clinics, etc.)
_____Doesn't feel he/she needs help
_____Received help but feels it did no good
_____Seeking help
_____Not sure what to do about it

VII. Family Strength

54. In the past month, have you had problems with your husband/wife?* Would you say (READ RESPONSES)

_____Almost never
_____Sometimes
_____Often
_____Almost always
_____Not applicable
_____Don't know

55. In the past month, have you had problems with your children? Would you say (READ RESPONSES)

_____Almost never
_____Sometimes
_____Often
_____Almost always
_____Not applicable
_____Don't know

56. In the past month, have you had problems with other family members? Would you say (READ RESPONSES)

_____Almost never
_____Sometimes
_____Often
_____Almost always
_____Not applicable
_____Don't know

57. In the past month, have you had problems raising children, taking care of their needs, training, discipline, etc.? Would you say (READ RESPONSES)

_____Almost never
_____Sometimes
_____Often
_____Almost always
_____Not applicable
_____Don't know

58. In the past month, have you had problems taking care of the house, meals, or family health matters? Would you say (READ RESPONSES)

_____Almost never
_____Sometimes
_____Often
_____Almost always
_____Not applicable
_____Don't know

59. In the past month, have you had problems managing money or with budgeting or credit? Would you say (READ RESPONSES)

_____Almost never
_____Sometimes
_____Often   } (ASK a)
_____Almost always)
_____Not applicable
_____Don't know

   a. What is the nature of the problem? _____
   _____

---

*In modern society, with the increasing prevalence of nonmarrieds living together, this term "husband/wife" probably should be broadened to include these other situations.

60. In the past month, did the members of your family have difficulty talking over problems, listening to each other, and sharing feelings? Would you say (READ RESPONSES)

_____Almost never
_____Sometimes
_____Often
_____Almost always
_____Not applicable
_____Don't know

61. In the past month, did the members of your family have problems handling arguments and working out differences? Would you say (READ RESPONSES)

_____Almost never
_____Sometimes
_____Often
_____Almost always
_____Not applicable
_____Don't know

62. In the past month, did the members of your family have problems feeling close to each other? Would you say (READ RESPONSES)

_____Almost never
_____Sometimes
_____Often
_____Almost always
_____Not applicable
_____Don't know

63. In the past month, have you had other family problems that we have not mentioned? Would you say (READ RESPONSES)

_____Almost never
_____Sometimes }
_____Often   } (ASK a)
_____Almost always }
_____Not applicable
_____Don't know

   a. What is the nature of the problem? _____
   _____

(ASK QUESTIONS 64-74 ONLY AT FOLLOW-UP)

64. What was your marital status at intake?

_____Single
_____Married
_____Separated
_____Divorced
_____Widowed

   a. What is your current marital status?

      _____Single
      _____Married
      _____Separated
      _____Divorced
      _____Widowed

   b. (DO NOT ASK IF RESPONDENT HAS BECOME "WIDOWED")
      Would you say you are more satisfied or less satisfied with your marital status now than you were at intake?

      _____More satisfied
      _____Somewhat more satisfied
      _____About the same
      _____Somewhat less satisfied
      _____Less satisfied

These next questions are about problems that you and your family had when you came to the (name of agency) and whether these problems are now much better, somewhat better, the same, somewhat worse, or much worse.

65. When you first came to (name of agency), did you have problems with your husband/wife?

_____Yes   (ASK *a*)
_____No   (GO TO NEXT QUESTION)

  a. Are these problems now (READ RESPONSES)

     _____Much better
     _____Somewhat better
     _____About the same
     _____Somewhat worse
     _____Much worse

66. When you first came to (name of agency), did you have problems with your children?

_____Yes   (ASK *a*)
_____No   (GO TO NEXT QUESTION)

  a. Are these problems now (READ RESPONSES)

     _____Much better
     _____Somewhat better
     _____About the same
     _____Somewhat worse
     _____Much worse

67. When you first came to (name of agency), did you have problems with other family members?

_____Yes   (ASK *a*)
_____No   (GO TO NEXT QUESTION)

  a. Are these problems now (READ RESPONSES)

     _____Much better
     _____Somewhat better
     _____About the same
     _____Somewhat worse
     _____Much worse

68. When you first came to (name of agency), did you have problems raising children, taking care of their needs, training, discipline, etc.?

_____Yes   (ASK *a*)
_____No   (GO TO NEXT QUESTION)

  a. Are these problems now (READ RESPONSES)

     _____Much better
     _____Somewhat better
     _____About the same
     _____Somewhat worse
     _____Much worse

69. When you first came to (name of agency), did you have problems taking care of the house, meals, or family health matters?

_____Yes   (ASK *a*)
_____No   (GO TO NEXT QUESTION)

  a. Are these problems now (READ RESPONSES)

     _____Much better
     _____Somewhat better
     _____About the same
     _____Somewhat worse
     _____Much worse

70. When you first came to (name of agency), did you have problems managing money or with budgeting or credit?

_____Yes (ASK *a*)
_____No   (GO TO NEXT QUESTION)

a. What was the nature of the problems? _____

_____

Are these problems now (READ RESPONSES)

_____Much better
_____Somewhat better
_____About the same
_____Somewhat worse
_____Much worse

71. Since you started getting help from (name of agency), has there been any change in the way the members of your family talk over problems, listen to each other, share feelings?

_____Yes (ASK *a*)
_____No   (GO TO NEXT QUESTION)

a. Would you say it is now (READ RESPONSES)

_____Much better
_____Somewhat better
_____Somewhat worse
_____Much worse
_____Not a problem

72. Since you started getting help from (name of agency), has there been any change in the way the members of your family handle arguments and work out differences?

_____Yes (ASK *a*)
_____No   (GO TO NEXT QUESTION)

a. Would you say it is now (READ RESPONSES)

_____Much better
_____Somewhat better
_____Somewhat worse
_____Much worse
_____Not a problem

73. Since you started getting help from (name of agency), has there been any change in the way the members of your family feel toward each other (how close and comfortable, how you enjoy each other)?

_____Yes (ASK *a*)
_____No   (GO TO NEXT QUESTION)

a. Would you say it is now (READ RESPONSES)

_____Much better
_____Somewhat better
_____Somewhat worse
_____Much worse
_____Not a problem

74. When you first came to (name of agency), did you have other major family problems that we have not mentioned?

_____ Yes   (ASK a)
_____ No   (GO TO NEXT QUESTION)

a. What was the nature of the problems? _____
    _____

    Are these problems now (READ RESPONSES)

    _____ Much better
    _____ Somewhat better
    _____ About the same
    _____ Somewhat worse
    _____ Much worse

VIII. Child Problem Behavior

75.* How many children do you have who are below the age of 18? What are their names and ages?

	Name	Age			Name	Age
a.	_____	_____		e.	_____	_____
b.	_____	_____		f.	_____	_____
c.	_____	_____		g.	_____	_____
d.	_____	_____		h.	_____	_____

76. In the past month, how often did (name of child) show anger by having tantrums? (READ RESPONSES)

_____Almost never
_____Sometimes
_____Often
_____Almost always

77. In the past month, how often did (name of child) fight or hurt peers when playing with them? (READ RESPONSES)

_____Almost never
_____Sometimes
_____Often
_____Almost always

78. In the past month, how often did (name of child) act withdrawn and uncommunicative? (READ RESPONSES)

_____Almost never
_____Sometimes
_____Often
_____Almost always

79. In the past month, how often did (name of child) steal things from others? (READ RESPONSES)

_____Almost never
_____Sometimes
_____Often
_____Almost always

80. In the past month, how often did (name of child) resist or refuse to do what was asked? (READ RESPONSES)

_____Almost never
_____Sometimes
_____Often
_____Almost always

81. In the past month, how often did (name of child) destroy property, commit vandalism? (READ RESPONSES)

_____Almost never
_____Sometimes
_____Often
_____Almost always

_____

*When there is more than one child, this group of questions should be administered for each child.

82. In the past month, how often did (name of child) play hooky? (READ RESPONSES)

_____Almost never
_____Sometimes
_____Often
_____Almost always

83. In the past month, did (name of child) ever run away from home?

_____Yes   How many times? _____
_____No

84. Was (name of child) arrested in the past twelve months?

_____Yes
_____No

85. Is (name of child) currently in school?

_____Yes   (ASK a AND b)
_____No   (GO TO NEXT QUESTION)

a. In the past twelve months, has (name of child)

_____Failed a course?
_____Failed a grade?
_____Been suspended or expelled?
_____None of the above

b. In the past month, have you had complaints from (name of child)'s teacher about behavior in class?

_____Almost never
_____Sometimes
_____Often
_____Almost always

(ASK QUESTIONS 86-92 ONLY AT FOLLOW-UP)

86. Since you started getting help from (name of agency), has there been a change in (name of child) with respect to showing anger by having tantrums?

_____Yes   (ASK a)
_____No   (GO TO NEXT QUESTION)

a. Would you say (name of child) is now (READ RESPONSES)

_____Much better
_____Somewhat better
_____About the same
_____Somewhat worse
_____Much worse

87. Since you started getting help from (name of agency), has there been a change in (name of child) with respect to fighting or hurting peers when playing with them?

_____Yes   (ASK a)
_____No   (GO TO NEXT QUESTION)

a. Would you say (name of child) is now (READ RESPONSES)

_____Much better
_____Somewhat better
_____About the same
_____Somewhat worse
_____Much worse

88. Since you started getting help from (name of agency), has there been a change in (name of child) with respect to acting withdrawn and uncommunicative?

_____Yes   (ASK *a*)
_____No   (GO TO NEXT QUESTION)

a. Would you say (name of child) is now (READ RESPONSES)

    _____Much better
    _____Somewhat better
    _____About the same
    _____Somewhat worse
    _____Much worse

89. Since you started getting help from (name of agency), has there been a change in (name of child) with respect to stealing things from others?

_____Yes   (ASK *a*)
_____No   (GO TO NEXT QUESTION)

a. Would you say (name of child) is now (READ RESPONSES)

    _____Much better
    _____Somewhat better
    _____About the same
    _____Somewhat worse
    _____Much worse

90. Since you started getting help from (name of agency), has there been a change in (name of child) with respect to resisting or refusing to do what is asked?

_____Yes   (ASK *a*)
_____No   (GO TO NEXT QUESTION)

a. Would you say (name of child) is now (READ RESPONSES)

    _____Much better
    _____Somewhat better
    _____About the same
    _____Somewhat worse
    _____Much worse

91. Since you started getting help from (name of agency), has there been a change in (name of child) with respect to destroying property, committing vandalism?

_____Yes   (ASK *a*)
_____No   (GO TO NEXT QUESTION)

a. Would you say (name of child) is now (READ RESPONSES)

    _____Much better
    _____Somewhat better
    _____About the same
    _____Somewhat worse
    _____Much worse

92. Since you started getting help from (name of agency), has there been a change in (name of child) with respect to playing hooky?

_____Yes   (ASK *a*)
_____No   (GO TO NEXT QUESTION)

a. Would you say (name of child) is now (READ RESPONSES)

    _____Much better
    _____Somewhat better
    _____About the same
    _____Somewhat worse
    _____Much worse

IX. Client Satisfaction

(ASK QUESTIONS 93-104 ONLY AT FOLLOW-UP)

93. What are the problems that led you to get help from (name of agency) since (date)?

    a._____

    b._____

    c._____

    d._____

94. Considering the problems that led you to get help from (name of agency), how would you say things are now?

    _____Much better
    _____Somewhat better
    _____About the same
    _____Somewhat worse
    _____Better in some ways but worse in others } (ASK *a*)

    a. Please explain: _____
    _____

95. Do you feel the help you received from (name of agency) influenced the changes you mentioned above?

    _____Helped a great deal
    _____Helped some
    _____Made no difference
    _____Made things worse   (ASK *a*)

    a. Please explain: _____
    _____

96. In general, how do you feel about the services provided by (name of agency) since (date)?

    _____Very satisfied
    _____Satisfied
    _____No particular feelings one way or the other
    _____Not satisfied   (ASK *a*)

    a. Please explain: _____
    _____

97. Did you have any problem with fees? Was there (READ RESPONSES)

    _____No problem
    _____A small problem }
    _____A major problem } (ASK *a*)
    _____Don't know

    a. Please explain: _____
    _____

98. Did you have any problem with waiting time for filling out forms, getting help, etc.? Was there (READ RESPONSES)

    _____No problem
    _____A small problem }
    _____A major problem } (ASK *a*)
    _____Don't know

    a. Please explain: _____
    _____

99. Did you have any problem with location of services? Was there (READ RESPONSES)

_____No problem
_____A small problem ⎫
_____A major problem ⎭ (ASK a)
_____Don't know

a. Please explain: _____
_____

100. Did you have any problem with appointment times with your caseworker? Was there (READ RESPONSES)

_____No problem
_____A small problem ⎫
_____A major problem ⎭ (ASK a)
_____Don't know

a. Please explain: _____
_____

101. Did you have any problem with changes in caseworkers? Was there (READ RESPONSES)

_____No problem
_____A small problem ⎫
_____A major problem ⎭ (ASK a)
_____Don't know

a. Please explain: _____
_____

102. Did you have any problem with paperwork? Was there (READ RESPONSES)

_____No problem
_____A small problem ⎫
_____A major problem ⎭ (ASK a)
_____Don't know

a. Please explain: _____
_____

103. Did you have any problem with the way caseworkers treated you? Was there (READ RESPONSES)

_____No problem
_____A small problem ⎫
_____A major problem ⎭ (ASK a)
_____Don't know

a. Please explain: _____
_____

104. Are there any other comments you would like to make about the quality of the services you received?

_____
_____
_____

X. Amenities of Care in Institutions

105. In the past two weeks, have your meals been served hot enough? (READ RESPONSES)

_____All of the time
_____Most of the time
_____Some of the time
_____Rarely

106. In the past two weeks, did you like the taste of the food served here? (READ RESPONSES)

_____All of the time
_____Most of the time
_____Some of the time
_____Rarely

107. In the past two weeks, did you get enough food to eat? (READ RESPONSES)

_____All of the time
_____Most of the time
_____Some of the time
_____Rarely

108. In the past two weeks, did you get clean sheets and towels often enough? (READ RESPONSES)

_____All of the time
_____Most of the time
_____Some of the time
_____Rarely

109. In the past two weeks, were your clothes washed often enough? (READ RESPONSES)

_____All of the time
_____Most of the time
_____Some of the time
_____Rarely

110. In the past two weeks, did you have sufficient opportunities to socialize with the other people who live here? (READ RESPONSES)

_____All of the time
_____Most of the time
_____Some of the time }
_____Rarely   } (ASK a)

a. Please explain: _____
    _____

111. In the past two weeks, have you had enough opportunities for recreation? (READ RESPONSES)

_____All of the time
_____Most of the time
_____Some of the time }
_____Rarely   } (ASK a)

a. Please explain: _____
    _____

112. In the past two weeks, when you wanted something done, did the staff members respond to your needs? (READ RESPONSES)

_____All of the time
_____Most of the time
_____Some of the time
_____Rarely

113. In the past two weeks, did the staff members treat you politely and with respect? (READ RESPONSES)

_____ All of the time
_____ Most of the time
_____ Some of the time }
_____ Rarely   } (ASK a)

a. Please explain: _____
   _____

114. In the past two weeks, did you get medical care when you needed it? (READ RESPONSES)

_____ All of the time
_____ Most of the time
_____ Some of the time }
_____ Rarely   } (ASK a)

a. Please explain: _____
   _____

115. Is there someone here to whom you can make an official complaint about something you don't like?

_____ Yes
_____ No
_____ Don't know

116. In the past year, have you make an official complaint about anything here?

_____ Yes (ASK a)
_____ No   (ASK b)

a. Was anything done about it?

   _____ Yes Please describe what happened: _____
   _____ No
   _____ Don't know

b. Do you know anyone who made an official complaint about something here during the past year?

   _____ Yes (ASK c)
   _____ No   (GO TO NEXT QUESTION)

c. Was anything done about it?

   _____ Yes Please describe what happened: _____
   _____ No
   _____ Don't know

117. In the past two weeks, have you like the way (name of institution) looked (appearance, cleanness, general maintenance)? (READ RESPONSES)

_____ All of the time
_____ Most of the time
_____ Some of the time }
_____ Rarely   } (ASK a)

a. Please explain: _____
   _____

118. In the past two weeks, was the temperature of your room comfortable? (READ RESPONSES)

_____ All of the time
_____ Most of the time
_____ Some of the time
_____ Rarely

119. In the past two weeks, has there been anything you especially liked about this place?

    _____

    _____

120. In the past two weeks, has there been anything you especially disliked about this place?

    _____

    _____

121. In general, to what extent are you satisfied with (name of institution)?   (READ RESPONSES)

    _____Very satisfied
    _____Satisfied
    _____Dissatisfied
    _____Very dissatisfied

122. (FOR THOSE WHO MOVED TO THE CURRENT INSTITUTION DURING THE PREVIOUS YEAR)
    How would you compare (name of institution) to where you were before?   (READ RESPONSES)

    _____Current place is far better
    _____Current place is somewhat better
    _____Current place is better in some ways and worse in others
    _____Current place is worse
    _____Don't know

    a. Please explain: _____

    _____

MISCELLANEOUS INFORMATION

The following information will often be obtained from case records or other government records.

Physical Health

R-1   Client has died

Mental Distress

R-2   Client committed suicide
R-3   Evidence of at least one incident of a nervous breakdown or attempted suicide

Alcohol and Drug Abuse

R-4   Evidence of at least one arrest or conviction related to use of alcohol during past three months
R-5   Evidence of at least one arrest or conviction related to use of drugs during past three months

Child Welfare

R-6   Frequency and severity of recurrence of abuse or neglect
      --No indication of child abuse or neglect
      --Reported but unconfirmed case of child abuse or neglect
      --Confirmed case of child abuse or neglect
      --Child removed from home temporarily due to recurrence of abuse or neglect
      --Child removed from home permanently due to recurrence of abuse or neglect
      --Injury to child resulting from abuse
      --Death of child as a result of abuse

R-7   Timeliness of placement
      --Child placed in adoptive home within ninety days after decision to seek adoptive placement
      --For "hard to place" child: Child placed in adoptive home within one year after decision
        to seek adoptive placement
      --Child's adoption legally completed within one year

R-8   Placement status
      --Improvement: Institution to own home
                          Foster home to own home
                          Institution to adoption
                          Foster home to adoption
                          Institution to foster home
      --No change: Continuing in own home
                          Continuing in foster home
                          Continuing in institution
                          Continuing in adoption
      --Deterioration: Changed foster home; foster parents unable to continue care
                          Changed foster home; incompatible foster home
                          Went from foster home to institution
                          Child transferred to another institution for reasons other than age or
                              improvement in conditions
                          Child placed in institution within twelve months of being discharged from
                              another institution (recidivism)

Appendix B

ILLUSTRATIVE SET OF QUESTIONS FOR CITIZEN SURVEYS OF UNMET NEED*

DEMOGRAPHIC QUESTIONS

First, I'd like to ask you for some general information about yourself and your household.

A. What is the postal Zip Code for your residence?**   _____Zip Code

B. What racial or ethnic group do you belong to?

_____Caucasian
_____Black
_____Oriental
_____Other (specify) _____

C. Who lives in your household? For each person, starting with yourself, please tell me their relationship, age, and sex.

Relationship to Respondent	Age	Sex	Relationship to Respondent	Age	Sex
a. Respondent	_____	_____	e._____	_____	_____
b._____	_____	_____	f._____	_____	_____
c._____	_____	_____	g._____	_____	_____
d._____	_____	_____	h._____	_____	_____

D. I will now read you a list of income ranges. Please tell me which range your total household gross income falls into?***

Yearly	Monthly
_____Under $2,000	_____Under $166
_____$2,000-3,999	_____$167-333
_____$4,000-5,999	_____$334-499
_____$6,000-7,999	_____$500-666
_____$8,000-9,999	_____$667-833
_____$10,000-14,999	_____$834-1,249
_____$15,000-19,999	_____$1,250-1,666
_____$20,000-29,999	_____$1,667-2,499
_____$30,000 and over	_____$2,500 and over
_____Don't know	
_____Refuses to answer	

_____

*Many of the questions suggested here were adapted from existing surveys (especially the New Hampshire Social Service Needs Survey conducted in early 1976--see Volume II, Chapter 9). See Chapter 5 of this volume for a discussion of the rationale for our choice of general approach and questions and for suggestions on administration of the survey.

**Zip Code is only one possible "location" indicator. Agencies using the survey may prefer to record town, county, region, or other location data.

***It has been found in some surveys that respondents are less reluctant to disclose income when it is handled in this way, with a request to specify a range rather than the exact income. A preface to the request for income may also be useful, with reassurance that the information will be used in aggregate form with no identification of the respondent. The interviewer may have to clarify "gross income" for a respondent, also.

NEEDS QUESTIONS

The following questions concern personal and family problems which people often have, and for which they might look for help from somewhere--family, friends, community agencies, family doctor, and so on. For each of these questions, I would like you to tell me whether you or any other members of your household have had the problem mentioned during the past year and, if so, to give me some information on whether you received any help with the problem.

1. In the past year, have you or any other members of your household had <u>financial</u> problems or difficulty in getting money which you needed?

   (Answer Module)

2. In the past year, have you or any other members of your household had problems with <u>employment</u>, such as difficulty finding work, dissatisfaction with your job, and the like?

   (Answer Module)

3. In the past year, have you or any other members of your household not been able to get adequate <u>medical and dental care</u> when you needed it?

   (Answer Module)

4. In the past year, have you or any other members of your household needed help <u>taking care of yourself</u> or themselves--for example, bathing, getting around the house, dressing, cooking, and so forth--but had no one living in your house who could give you enough help?

   (Answer Module)

5. In the past year, have you or any other members of your household been so <u>burdened with the care of someone else</u> that you were unable to take good care of them or that you had to give up activities, such as work, which you were unhappy about giving up?

   (Answer Module)

6. In the past year, have you or any other members of your household <u>felt unhappy</u> enough with yourself or your life situation that you or they thought of getting help--like some sort of counseling--with the problems?

   (Answer Module)

7. In the past year, have you or any other members of your household been <u>mentally ill, retarded, or senile</u>?

   (Answer Module)

8. In the past year, has <u>your family had troubles</u> such as fights, lack of communication among family members, trouble in cooperating on chores, and so forth, to the extent that you or others thought of getting help with the family problems?

   (Answer Module)

9. In the past year, have you or any other members of your household had a <u>drinking</u> problem?*

   (Answer Module)

---

*Drinking, drug abuse, and child abuse and neglect are problems to which many people may not admit on a survey. There are scales designed to elicit information related to these problems--for instance, a list of questions on parents' attitudes toward their children and punishment--which try to find out about the existence of a problem without asking directly. However, since they are comparatively long and their validity is largely undemonstrated, they are not included here. Groups using the questionnaire might wish, however, to substitute or add these scales into the questionnaire for their own use.

ANSWER MODULE

For each problem area, the respondent is asked whether any members of the household have had the problem. If the answer is "yes," the identity of the household member(s) who have had the problem is recorded and a series of questions is asked for each person with the problem. (Note: In the coded lists of "reasons," the responses labeled "N" are reasons which are relatively noncontrollable by government action; those labeled "C" are relatively controllable, while those labeled "?" may be either.)

☐ No problem   ☐ Yes

a. Household member:

_____ / _____ / _____
Relationship/Age/Sex

b. How important was this problem?

CODE
1. Minor
2. Moderate
3. Major

c. Did you/he/she try to get help for this problem?

☐ No   ☐ Yes

d. Why not?   e. What kind of help did you/he/she try to get?

_____

CODE

N
1. Could handle problem without help
2. No one else could help with problem
3. Didn't want to go to outsiders
4. Didn't want public help
5. Too busy

f. From whom?

CODE
1. Agency
2. Private counselor, minister, doctor, etc.
3. Friend or family
4. Other_____
5. Don't know

C
6. Thought no help was available
7. Thought couldn't afford help
8. Thought not eligible
9. Didn't know how to find help
10. Transportation problem
11. No one to care for child/other family member temporarily

?
12. Other_____
_____
13. Don't know

g. Did you/he/she receive some help?

☐ No   ☐ Yes

h. Why not?   i. What help did you/he/she receive?

_____

CODE

C
1. Couldn't find help
2. Couldn't afford help
3. Not eligible
4. Transportation problem
5. No one to care for child/other family member temporarily

?
6. Other_____
_____
7. Don't know

j. Were you/he/she satisfied with the help received?

☐ No   ☐ Yes

k. Why not?

_____

GO ON TO NEXT HOUSEHOLD MEMBER OR NEXT PROBLEM.

10. In the past year, have you or any other members of your household had a problem with drugs?

(Answer Module)

11. In the past year, have you or any other members of your household felt that you didn't have enough social contact with other people, or did not have enough to do in your leisure time?

(Answer Module)

12. In the past year, have you or any other members of your household had any problems with the children in the family--behavior problems, conflict between yourselves and the children, school problems, and so on?

(Answer Module)

13. In the past year, have you or any other members of your household needed daytime child care but had trouble getting it or affording it?

(Answer Module)

14. In the past year, have you or any other members of your household wished either to have more children or prevent having more children but had difficulty doing so?

(Answer Module)

15. In the past year, have you or any other members of your household had transportation problems, such as trouble getting around due to disability, lack of a car or bus service, and the like?

(Answer Module)

16. In the past year, have you or any other members of your household had problems with housing, such as not enough room, trouble getting repairs, feeling unsafe in the neighborhood, and so forth?

(Answer Module)

17. In the past year, have you or any other members of your household had any problems other than those we've mentioned?

Problem: _____ (Answer Module)

Problem: _____ (Answer Module)

Appendix C

A BRIEF REVIEW OF SOME PAST SOCIAL SERVICES
EVALUATION ACTIVITIES

This Appendix briefly summarizes some of the principal directions of past evaluation approaches. A detailed review of these evaluative and analytical efforts will be found in Volume II.[1]

The five goals of Title XX, ambiguous and overlapping as they are, are a useful way to sort out the various studies and evaluation efforts conducted hitherto on the outcomes of social services.

Goal 1 - achieving or maintaining economic self-support to prevent, reduce, or eliminate dependency. The principal procedures found were follow-ups of clients after case closure to determine the extent of economic self-support achieved. Two relevant efforts are of particular interest. The first is the evaluation conducted by the U.S. General Accounting Office in 1973 of the degree to which welfare recipients achieved self-support or reduced dependency. Although criticized at the time on a number of grounds, the GAO study provides a useful illustration of how client follow-up as to employment and earnings might be undertaken, including identification of an employability assessment tool (the "Denver Inventory") that might be used at intake to characterize clients by difficulty. The second work is that of the state of Oklahoma's "Services Outcome Measurement" (SOM) procedure to assess client change and difficulty. This procedure, oriented to vocational rehabilitation, makes use of a tested instrument for rating client functioning at entry and at case closure.

Goal 2 - achieving or maintaining self-sufficiency, including reduction or prevention of dependency.[2] There appear to be two main types of procedures for estimating the degree of client improvement relating to self-sufficiency.

The first is the use of a predetermined set of "functioning characteristics" on which the client is rated. This has usually been done either by having a trained observer rate the client or by interviewing the client, using in both cases a questionnaire based on the relevant functioning characteristics.

_____

1. Bibliographical references for the studies mentioned in this Appendix are identified in the selected bibliography.

2. We have interpreted Goal 2 as relating to adult self-sufficiency, leaving child dependency issues to be discussed under Goal 3.

The Barthel Index, the HEW Patient Classification System, the Katz Index of Independence in Activities of Daily Living, and the Duke University Older Americans Multi-Dimensional Functional Assessment Scale are all examples of client-functioning ratings through use of a predetermined set of functioning characteristics. These sets were developed primarily for the aged and chronically ill or disabled persons. Their focus on functioning and behavioral variables, instead of symptomatic or diagnostic ones, has several advantages. Functioning and behavioral variables are easier for public officials to understand and are more amenable to observation and measurement. The procedures have been subjected to some testing. Any state using them, however, should conduct additional reliability-validation tests.

The second approach is to obtain the client's own perceptions of the degree of improvement. This has been used in a number of studies, including the procedures developed by the Family Service Association of America for evaluating family-counseling services and by the Bureau of Social Welfare in Maine. There is some controversy about the validity of client assessment of change. The client might feel helped, whereas an "objective" observer might find the opposite to be true. Our perspective is that the two approaches are complementary and should both be used.

Goal 3 - preventing or limiting abuse, neglect, or exploitation of children and adults unable to protect their own interests, or preserving, rehabilitating, or reuniting families. This goal has several parts. Information on the incidence and recidivism of child (or adult) abuse, potentially available from government records, is relevant here. In addition, it seems appropriate to attempt to assess the children's status relevant to the attempted amelioration of problems that neglected and abused problem-children have. Examples of procedures that have been undertaken, at least on an ad hoc basis, are the Wisconsin program audit of foster home care, the North Carolina Mental Health Division study of residential treatment facilities, and the St. Aemilian Child Care Center study (Wisconsin). The latter utilized two child behavior rating scales (the "Devereux Child Behavior Rating Scale" and the "Devereux Elementary School Behavior Rating Scale") to assess the effects of a residential treatment center on the behavior of boys between the ages of seven and thirteen.

For assessing status relative to family health and functioning, one approach is to use the Geismar Family Functioning Assessment. Unfortunately, the procedure is complex and involves considerable rater subjectivity.[1] An alternative to the Geismar procedure is the Family Service Association of America procedure utilizing client responses to questions about their perceptions of varius aspects of the quality of their family life. "Objective" indicators such as separation and divorce status can also be used, but these only indicate status and not whether the status is satisfactory. Thus, when indicators of marital status are used, feedback from clients as to their satisfaction with a particular status also seems necessary.

---

1. For example, the procedure calls for the rating of twenty-six items grouped into such areas as Family Relations and Family Unity, Individual Behavior and Adjustment, and others.

Goal 4 - preventing or reducing inappropriate institutional care by providing for community-based care, home-based care, or other forms of less intensive care. "Appropriateness of placement" is a surrogate concept for the real aim of helping clients to live as pleasantly and as self-sufficiently as possible (and at the least possible cost). Information on client functioning (such as the ability to undertake activities of daily living) obtained for the previous goals can be combined with information on the availability of resources in the community (public and private) in order to obtain a set of criteria for rating the appropriateness of institutionalization. A study by the Greater London Council in 1972 on assessing the need of the elderly for residential care is an example of such an approach.

Goal 5 - securing referral for admission to institutional care when other forms of care are not appropriate, or providing services to individuals in institutions. The procedures for Goal 4 are also relevant here in order to estimate the need of current clients for institutionalization. The difference is that in this case the need for institutionalization is the focus of interest.

It also seems necessary to estimate the number, or percentage, of persons in the state needing institutionalization who are not receiving social services. One possible approach to this is a statewide survey of a representative cross section of the population, such as the social service surveys used by the states of Florida, New Jersey, and New Hampshire. Such a survey can simultaneously obtain data on the extent of unmet needs related to other goals, such as economic help (Goal 1), self-sufficiency (Goal 2), and family strength (Goal 3). Goal 5 also involves the provision of adequate care to those who are currently institutionalized. It seems necessary, therefore, to assess the adequacy and quality of care provided to them, although Title XX itself does not in general provide funds for such care. Possible procedures include the use of trained observers or interviews of the clients themselves.

SELECTED BIBLIOGRAPHY

Babbie, Earl R. Survey Research Methods. Belmont, Calif.: Wadsworth Publishing Company, 1973.

Beck, Dorothy Fahs. "Research Findings on the Outcomes of Marital Counseling." Social Casework, March 1975.

Beck, Dorothy Fahs, and Jones, Mary Ann. How To Conduct a Client Follow-Up Study. New York: Family Service Association of America, 1974.

_____. "A New Look at Clientele and Services of Family Agencies." Social Casework, December 1974.

_____. Progress on Family Problems: A Nationwide Study of Clients' and Counselors' Views on Family Agency Services. New York: Family Service Association of America, 1973.

Blair, Louis H., and Sessler, John. Drug Program Assessment. Washington, D.C.: The Drug Abuse Council, February 1974.

Brown, Gordon E., ed. The Multi-Problem Dilemma: A Social Research Demonstration with Multi-Problem Families. Metuchen, N.J.: The Scarecrow Press, 1968.

Buros, Oscar Krisen, ed. The Seventh Mental Measurements Yearbook. 2 vols. Highland Park, N.J.: Gryphon Press, 1972.

Catholic Social Service, Diocese of La Crosse, Wis. "A Survey of Counseling Effectiveness as Perceived by Clients." June 1974.

Ciarlo, James A., and Reihman, Jacqueline. "The Denver Community Mental Health Questionnaire: Development of a Multi-Dimensional Program Evaluation Instrument." Denver, Colo.: Mental Health Systems Evaluation Project of the Northwest Denver Mental Health Center and the University of Denver, 1974.

Davis, Howard R. "Four Ways to Goal Attainment: An Overview." Evaluation 1, no. 2 (1973).

Derogatis, Leonard R.; Lipman, Ronald S.; and Covi, Lino. "SCL-90: An Outpatient Psychiatric Rating Scale--Preliminary Report." Psychopharmacology Bulletin 9 (1973):13-28.

Derogatis, Leonard R.; Lipman, Ronald S.; Rickels, Karl; Uhlenhuth, E.H.; and Covi, Lino. "The Hopkins Symptom Checklist (HSCL): A Self-Report Symptom Inventory." Behavioral Science 19, no. 1 (January 1974):1-15.

Duke University Center for the Study of Aging and Human Development, Older Americans Resources and Services Program. "OARS Multidimensional Functional Assessment Questionnaire." Durham, N.C., April 1975.

Ewing, J., and Rouse, B. "Identifying the 'Hidden Alcoholic.'" Paper presented at the 29th International Congress on Alcoholism and Drug Dependence, Sydney, Australia, February 2-6, 1970.

Florida, Department of Health and Rehabilitative Services. "Statewide Systematic Needs Assessment: SNAP Interview." 1976.

_____. Assessment of Needs of Low-Income, Urban Elderly Persons in the Florida Counties of Dade, Pinellas, and Palm Beach. May 1973.

Geismar, Ludwig L. Family and Community Functioning: A Manual of Measurement for Social Work Practice and Policy. Metuchen, N.J.: The Scarecrow Press, 1971.

Gueron, J., and Ouyang, B. "UI-MCTAB: A Multiple Crosstab Program." Washington, D.C.: The Urban Institute, August 8, 1974.

Katz, Sidney; Ford, Amasa B.; Moskowitz, Roland W.; Jackson, Beverly A.; and Jaffe, Marjorie W. "Studies of Illness in the Aged, The Index of ADL: A Standardized Measure of Biological and Psychosocial Function." Journal of the American Medical Association 185, no. 12 (September 21, 1963): 914-19.

Katz, Sidney; Ford, Amasa B.; Downs, Thomas D.; Adams, Mary; and Rusby, Dorothy I. The Effects of Continued Care: A Study of Chronic Illness in the Home. DHEW pub. no. (HSM) 73-3010, December 1972.

Kiresuk, Thomas, and Sherman, Robert. "Goal Attainment Scaling: A General Method for Evaluating Comprehensive Community Mental Health Programs." Community Mental Health Journal 4, no. 6 (1968).

Langner, T.S. "A Twenty-Two Item Screening Score of Psychiatric Symptoms Indicating Impairment." Journal of Health and Human Behavior 3 (1962): 269-76.

Lawton, M. Powell, and Brody, Elaine M. "Assessment of Older People: Self-Maintaining and Instrumental Activities of Daily Living." The Gerontologist 9, no. 3 (Autumn 1969):179-86.

Leighton, Dorothea C.; Harding, John S.; Macklin, David B.; Macmillan, Allister M.; and Leighton, Alexander H. The Character of Danger: Psychiatric Symptoms in Selected Communities. New York: Basic Books, 1963.

Lingren, Ronald H. "The Effects of a Residential Treatment Center Program Upon the Behaviors of Boys Aged 7-13: St. Aemilian Child Care Center." 2 vols. Milwaukee, Wis.: St. Aemilian Research Study, 1973.

Macmillan, Allister M. "The Health Opinion Survey: Technique for Estimating Prevalence of Psychoneurotic and Related Types of Disorder in Communities." Psychological Reports 3, supp. 7 (1957).

Mahoney, Florence I., and Barthel, Dorothea W. "Functional Evaluation: The Barthel Index." Maryland State Medical Journal, February 1965.

Maine, Department of Health and Welfare, Bureau of Social Welfare. An Evaluation of Contracted Social Services: Final Report, by Social Systems Research Corporation. February 15, 1975.

Maine, Department of Health and Welfare, Bureau of Social Welfare, Research, Evaluation and Planning Unit. Service Impact Analysis: A Report of the Study, by Mark S. Stein. 1972.

Manis, Jerome G.; Brawer, Milton J.; Hunt, Chester L.; and Kercher, Leonard C. "Validating a Mental Health Scale." American Sociological Review 28, no. 1 (February 1963):108-16.

Mayfield, Demmie; McLeod, Gail; and Hall, Patricia. "The CAGE Questionnaire: Validation of a New Alcoholism Screening Instrument." American Journal of Psychiatry 131, no. 10 (October 1974):1121-3.

Morse, Harold A. "Measuring the Potential of AFDC Families for Economic Independence." Welfare in Review 6, no. 6 (1968):13-18.

North Carolina, Division of Mental Health Services. "A Preliminary Glance at Residential Treatment Facilities for Children and Youth," by Jean H. Thrasher, Harold A. Berdiansky, Samuel N. Chasten, Lee D. Kittredge, and C. David Stephens. Working Paper no. 29. June 1975.

Northwest Federation for Human Services. "Microdata Sampling Systems: A Proposed Measurement Design." Boise, Idaho, April 19, 1976.

Nunnally, Jim. "The Study of Change in Evaluation Research." In Handbook of Evaluation Research. Edited by Marcia Guttentag and Elmer L. Struening, vol. 1, p. 112. Beverly Hills, Calif.: Sage Publications, 1975.

Ohio, Department of Mental Health and Mental Retardation. "Implementation Manual: Peer Review System for Public Mental Hospitals." October 31, 1974.

Oklahoma, Department of Institutions, Social and Rehabilitative Services. Case Difficulty and Client Change: Outcome Measurement. 4 monographs, by William J. Westerheide, Lowell Lenhart, and M. Clinton Miller III. 1974, 1975.

Pacific Consultants. "Service-Generic Evaluation of the Effectiveness of Social Services: Final Report." Berkeley, Calif.: Pacific Consultants, May 1975.

Riley, Patrick V. "Practice Changes Based on Research Findings." Social Casework, April 1975.

Schuerman, John R. "Do Family Services Help? An Essay Review." Social Services Review, September 1975.

Slonim, Morris J. Sampling in a Nutshell. New York: Simon and Schuster, 1960.

Speer, David C. "An Evaluation of the Denver Community Mental Health Questionnaire as a Measure of Outpatient Treatment Effectiveness." Columbus, Ind.: Quinco Consulting Center, 1976.

Spivack, George, and Spotts, Jules. Devereux Child Behavior Rating Scale Manual. Devon, Pa.: The Devereux Foundation, 1966.

Srole, Leo; Langner, Thomas S.; Michael, Stanley T.; Opler, Marvin K.; and Rennie, Thomas A.C. Mental Health in the Metropolis: The Midtown Manhattan Study. New York: McGraw-Hill, 1962.

Thompson, Quentin. "Assessing the Need for Residential Care for the Elderly." Quarterly Bulletin of the Intelligence Unit (Greater London Council), no. 24 (September 1973), pp. 37-42.

Turem, J.; Benton, B.; Dunlop, B.; and Millar, R. "Planning for Social Services: The Title XX Experience." Working Paper 0990-01. Washington, D.C.: The Urban Institute, October 1975.

U.S., Department of Health, Education and Welfare, Health Resources Administration. Patient Classification for Long-Term Care: User's Manual, by Ellen W. Jones. Washington, D.C.: DHEW pub. no. HRA 74-3107, December 1973.

U.S., Department of Health, Education and Welfare, National Institute of Mental Health. Handbook of Psychiatric Rating Scales. 2nd ed. Washington, D.C.: DHEW pub. no. (HSM) 73-9061, 1973.

_____. A Model for Estimating Mental Health Needs Using 1970 Census Socioeconomic Data. NIMH Series C, no. 9. 1974.

U.S., Department of Health, Education and Welfare, Public Health Service. "Quality Control and Measurement of Nonsampling Error in the Health Interview Survey." Vital and Health Statistics, series 2, no. 54.

U.S., Department of Health, Education and Welfare, Social and Rehabilitation Service. "Social Services Effectiveness: Evaluation of Alternative Measures and their Potential for Implementation." Washington, D.C., October 31, 1975.

_____. Social Services Effectiveness Study: A "Service-Generic" Evaluation of the Effectiveness of Social Services. 1976.

U.S., Executive Office of the President, Bureau of the Budget. Household Survey Manual, 1969. Washington, D.C., 1970.

U.S., General Accounting Office, Comptroller General. Social Services: Do They Help Welfare Recipients Achieve Self-Support or Reduced Dependency? Report to the Congress. June 27, 1973.

_____. Standards for Audit of Governmental Organizations, Programs, Activities, and Functions. Washington, D.C., 1972.

University of Denver, Center for Social Research and Development. Analysis and Synthesis of Needs Assessment Research in the Field of Human Services. Denver, 1974.

University of Wisconsin-Extension, Wisconsin Survey Research Laboratory. Statewide Citizens Survey. Questionnaire. Fall 1976.

Ward, James H.; Gutierrez, Fredrick; Most, Shira; Ostrander, Susan; and Smith, Paula. An Evaluation Prospectus for Measuring the Effectiveness of Social Services: Interim Report. Cleveland, Ohio: Case Western Reserve University, Human Services Design Laboratory, January 1976.

Ward, James H.; Gutierrez, Fredrick; Ostrander, Susan A.; and Most, Shira. Measuring the Effectiveness of Social Services: Final First Year Report. Cleveland, Ohio: Case Western Reserve University, Human Services Design Laboratory, July 1976.

Weiss, Carol H., and Hatry, Harry P. An Introduction to Sample Surveys for Government Managers. Washington, D.C.: The Urban Institute, 1971.

Wimberger, Herbert C., and Gregory, Robert J. "A Behavior Checklist for Use in Child Psychiatry Clinics." Journal of the American Academy of Child Psychiatry 7 (1968):677-88.

Wisconsin, Department of Health and Social Services. Predictors of Success in Foster Care, by Patricia W. Cautley and Martha J. Aldridge. August 1973.

Wisconsin, Department of Health and Social Services, Division of Mental Hygiene. "Client-Specific Program Evaluation: Goal Attainment Scaling (GAS)." Rev. 1975.

Wisconsin, Legislative Audit Bureau. "Audit Report of the Department of Health and Social Services Direct Services Foster Care Program." June 10, 1974.

Wolins, Martin, and Piliavin, Irving. Institution or Foster Family: A Century of Debate. New York: Child Welfare League of America, 1964.